Critical & CREATIVE Thinking Activities

Grade 4

Author: Rachel Lynette
Editor: Marilyn Evans
Copy Editing: Carrie Gwynne
Art Direction: Cheryl Puckett
Cover Illustration: Nathan Jarvis
Design/Production: Yuki Meyer

EMC 3394

Evan-Moor
EDUCATIONAL PUBLISHERS®
Helping Children Learn since 1979

Congratulations on your purchase of some of the finest teaching materials in the world.

Correlated
to State Standards

Photocopying the pages in this book is permitted for <u>single-classroom use only</u>. Making photocopies for additional classes or schools is prohibited.

Visit *teaching-standards.com* to view a correlation of this book's activities to your state's standards. This is a free service.

CONTENTS

What's in This Book?

Critical and Creative Thinking Activities, Grade 4 contains 46 themes, each presented in a three-page unit that gives students valuable practice with a broad range of thinking skills. The engaging themes will keep students interested and will have them begging to do the next set of activities!

The first and second pages of each unit get students thinking about the topic in a variety of ways. They may be asked to draw on prior knowledge or to generate new ideas.

The last page of each unit features one of a number of stimulating and entertaining formats, including logic puzzles, riddles, and secret codes.

How to Use This Book

• Use the activity pages during your language arts period to keep the rest of the class actively and productively engaged while you work with small groups of students.

• The themed sets of activity pages provide a perfect language arts supplement for your thematic or seasonal units. And you'll find any number of topics that complement your science and social studies curricula.

• Your students will enjoy doing these fun pages for homework or as free-time activities in class.

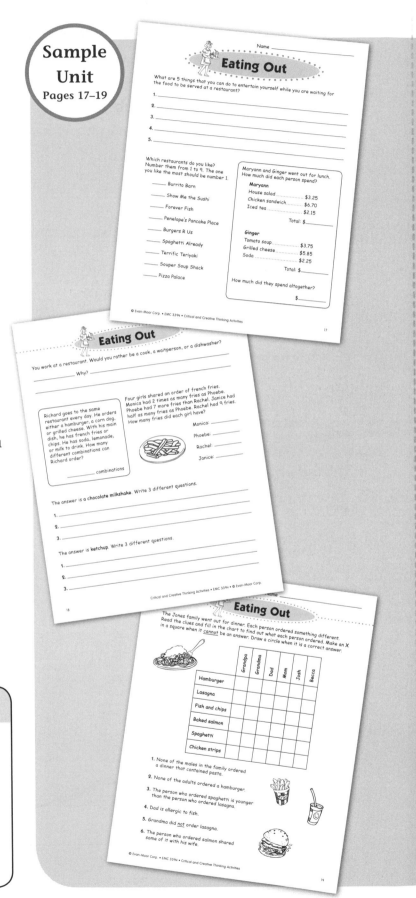

Sample Unit
Pages 17–19

About the Correlations for This Book

The valuable thinking skills practiced in this book (see inside front cover) are not generally addressed in state standards. However, thinking skills require content to be practiced. The activities in this book have been correlated to the Language Arts and Mathematics standards.

Visit www.teaching-standards.com to view a correlation of this book to your state's standards.

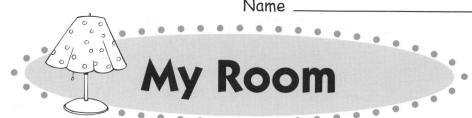

My Room

Write 6 adjectives to describe your room.

1. _____   3. _____   5. _____

2. _____   4. _____   6. _____

Unscramble these things that you would probably find in a bedroom. Then write the words in the grid.

DEB _____

KEDS _____

OROD _____

SKOBO _____

WILOPL _____

LETCOS _____

DONWWI _____

SLESVEH _____

SERRDES _____

STEHLOC _____

If there were a fire and you could save only 3 things from your room, what would you save?

1. _____

2. _____

3. _____

My Room

Some kids share a room with a brother or a sister. Write 3 advantages and 3 disadvantages of sharing a room.

Advantages	Disadvantages

ANALOGIES

shelves : books :: closet : _____

desk : study :: bed : _____

posters : wall :: rug : _____

pillow : soft :: desk : _____

If these things could talk, what would they say?

Your floor: _____

Your closet: _____

Your alarm clock: _____

Your pillow: _____

Rate your room.

messy   1 ---- 2 ---- 3 ---- 4 ---- 5   neat

boring   1 ---- 2 ---- 3 ---- 4 ---- 5   interesting

uncomfortable   1 ---- 2 ---- 3 ---- 4 ---- 5   comfortable

My Room

Use the clues to solve the crossword puzzle. The words are all things that can be found in a bedroom.

DOWN
1 Place for clothes
3 On the bed
4 Read this
7 On the wall
9 Has drawers
11 Put it together
13 Open it to leave
14 On the floor
15 Place for books
18 Where you sleep

ACROSS
2 Light up the room
5 Play with this
6 Tell the time
8 See outside
10 Prize for winning
12 Dirty clothes go here
13 Do homework here
15 For your feet
16 Play it with a friend
17 Nice to hug

Name _____

My School

How are your school and your home the same? How are they different?
Fill in the chart with 3 ways for each.

Same	Different

What is something that you really like about your school?

_____

What is something that you would change about your school if you could?

_____

How many times was Jordon late for school? He was late more than 8 times but fewer than 14 times. The number of times he was late is <u>not</u> divisible by 3. It is <u>not</u> an odd number.

Jordon was late

_____ times.

Write 2 **school** things for each letter.

D: _____ and _____

P: _____ and _____

B: _____ and _____

T: _____ and _____

C: _____ and _____

S: _____ and _____

W: _____ and _____

Name _____

My School

Use the groups of 3 letters on the right to complete the words on the left. The words are all things you are likely to find in a classroom.

B_____

TA_____

TEAC_____

PEN_____

CL_____

D_____

STAP_____

S_____

CRA_____

SHEL_____

CH_____

STUD_____

SCISS_____

G_____

INK

ENT

ORS

YON

LER

OOK

OCK

AIR

ESK

LUE

BLE

CIL

HER

VES

Read the clues. Match each student with his or her teacher.

• Abby and Cassie both have male teachers.

• Nathan's teacher is a woman. So is Katie's teacher.

• Jonah's teacher has only one syllable in her name.

• Katie's teacher's name begins with an **O**.

• Cassie's teacher has 5 letters in his name.

• Elliot's teacher's name has 6 letters in it.

Ms. Katz _____

Mr. Smith _____

Mrs. Oaks _____

Mr. Watson _____

Mrs. Kimbers _____

Mr. Olliver _____

Write a sentence about your school. Use exactly 12 words.

_____

_____

My School

The teacher has given you the job of assigning seats.
She has also given you a list of rules to follow.
Use the rules to fill in the seating chart.

- There must be 2 boys and 2 girls in each group.

- Students whose names begin with the same letter may not sit together.

- Students whose names end in **y** may not sit together.

- Students with 4 letters in their names may not sit together.

- Mitch, Tim, Jake, Andrew, Raul, and Derek must each be in a separate group.

- Amber, Kim, Sarah, and Jason each need to sit in one of the 2 groups nearest the front.

Students

Girls	Boys
Alison	Mitch
Emma	Tim
Shelby	Jake
Irene	Andrew
Gabby	Raul
Amber	Derek
Kim	Elliot
Lydia	Colby
Tara	Jason
Molly	Chad
Cassie	Sammy
Sarah	Marcus

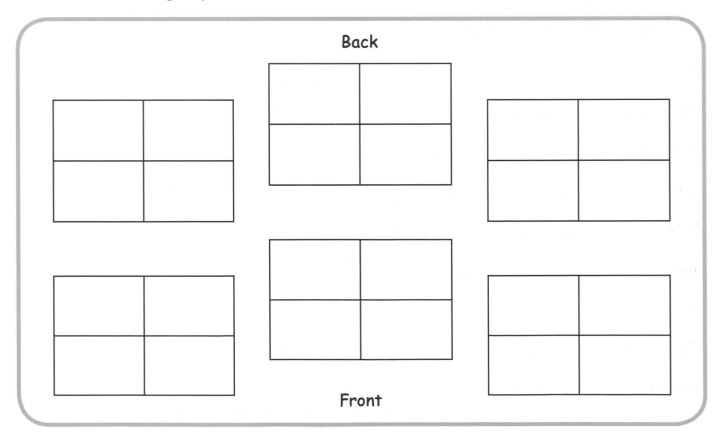

Back

Front

The Supermarket

Write a sentence that is always true about the supermarket.

_____

Write a sentence that is sometimes true about the supermarket.

_____

Write a sentence that is never true about the supermarket.

_____

You get to do the grocery shopping! The only rule is that you must buy one thing from each of the sections listed below. What do you buy?

Dairy _____

Cereal _____

Produce _____

Beverages _____

Cookies _____

Meat _____

Freezer _____

Chips _____

Bakery _____

Circle the better deal each time.

Apples
   3 for $1.00   or   5 for $1.75

Toilet paper
   3 rolls for $1.50   or   12 rolls for $5.25

Candy bars
   4 for $1.50   or   6 for $2.00

Why do you think stores often have candy and gum at the checkout stand?

_____

_____

_____

Name _____

The Supermarket

Marge bought 3 times as many groceries as Hilda. Edith bought half as many groceries as Hilda. Cora bought 4 times as many groceries as Edith. Marge bought 24 items at the grocery store. How many items did each woman buy?

Marge: _____

Hilda: _____

Edith: _____

Cora: _____

How many items did they buy altogether?

_____ items

ANAGRAMS

Use the letters in each of the words below to make a new word. The word you make must be something you can find at the grocery store.

TEAM _____

BEARD _____

MUG _____

LAST _____

LUMPS _____

SMILE _____

AUNT _____

Which of these is most like a supermarket: a pet store, a restaurant, or a bookstore?

_____ Why? _____

_____

ANALOGIES

yogurt : dairy :: banana : _____

cereal : box :: applesauce : _____

shopping cart : aisle :: car : _____

food : supermarket :: books : _____

Critical and Creative Thinking Activities • EMC 3394 • © Evan-Moor Corp.

Name _____

The Supermarket

You are doing the grocery shopping! You must do your shopping in the most efficient way possible. You may go through the store <u>only</u> once, and you can't cross your own path. First, look at the map of the store and rewrite the shopping list to show the order you would select each item. Then draw your path through the store.

Shopping List

- Cheerios
- Oreos
- Cheddar cheese
- Soda
- Tomato soup
- Ground beef
- Apple juice
- Brownie mix
- Ice-cream bars
- Bananas
- Hamburger buns
- Milk
- Can of corn
- Onions
- Rice krispies
- Graham crackers

Shopping List

_____   _____

_____   _____

_____   _____

_____   _____

_____   _____

_____   _____

_____   _____

_____   _____

Door In   **Door Out**

Checkout

Produce

Cookies, crackers, chips

Beverages

Cereal, baking

Soup, canned goods

Ice cream, frozen foods

Bakery

Meat

Dairy

At the Dinner Table

Think about the table where you usually eat dinner.

What shape is it? _____ How many legs does it have? _____

What is it made out of? _____

When you sit at your usual spot at the table, what do you see…

straight ahead? _____

to the left? _____

to the right? _____

Where does each person sit? Label the chairs.

• Mom sits at the west end of the table, and Dad sits at the east end of the table.

• The twins, Lily and Susie, sit across from each other.

• Grandma sits to the left of Dad.

• Ben sits next to Susie.

• Lily sits to the right of Mom.

Dinnertime is a good time to catch up with your family. What are 3 questions you could ask to make dinnertime more interesting?

1. _____

2. _____

3. _____

Critical and Creative Thinking Activities • EMC 3394 • © Evan-Moor Corp.

At the Dinner Table

Dad made baked potatoes. If he puts 1 potato on everyone's plate, he will have one extra potato. If he puts 2 potatoes on everyone's plate, one person will not get any potatoes at all. How many people are in Dad's family, and how many baked potatoes did he make?

_____ people

_____ potatoes

Julia's family eats rice with dinner every third night. They have peas every fourth night. It is Monday night, and Julia's family is eating both rice and peas. On what day of the week will they next eat rice and peas in the same meal?

_____

What are 5 other things you could use the dinner table for besides eating?

1. _____

2. _____

3. _____

4. _____

5. _____

Create the most disgusting dinner that you can imagine.

Main dish: _____

Side dish: _____

Vegetable: _____

Beverage: _____

Would you eat the dinner that you created for $100?

_____

What is the most disgusting thing that you have ever eaten?

_____

Name _____

At the Dinner Table

It's Rainbow Week at the Smith house! During Rainbow Week, the family eats a different color meal each night. Each meal must contain a main dish, a side dish, a vegetable, and a beverage. Every item must be the correct color. Can you think of a menu for each night?

	Main Dish	Side Dish	Vegetable	Beverage
Monday yellow				
Tuesday red				
Wednesday green				
Thursday brown				
Friday orange				
Saturday white				
Sunday purple				

Which night's dinner menu is your favorite? _____

Would you want to have Rainbow Week at your house? _____

Why or why not? _____

Eating Out

What are 5 things that you can do to entertain yourself while you are waiting for the food to be served at a restaurant?

1. _____

2. _____

3. _____

4. _____

5. _____

Which restaurants do you like? Number them from 1 to 9. The one you like the most should be number 1.

_____ Burrito Barn

_____ Show Me the Sushi

_____ Forever Fish

_____ Penelope's Pancake Place

_____ Burgers R Us

_____ Spaghetti Already

_____ Terrific Teriyaki

_____ Souper Soup Shack

_____ Pizza Palace

Maryann and Ginger went out for lunch. How much did each person spend?

Maryann

House salad $3.25

Chicken sandwich.......... $6.70

Iced tea $2.15

Total: $_____

Ginger

Tomato soup.................. $3.75

Grilled cheese.............. $5.85

Soda $2.25

Total: $_____

How much did they spend altogether?

$_____

Eating Out

You work at a restaurant. Would you rather be a cook, a waitperson, or a dishwasher?

_____ Why? _____

_____

Richard goes to the same restaurant every day. He orders either a hamburger, a corn dog, or grilled cheese. With his main dish, he has french fries or chips. He has soda, lemonade, or milk to drink. How many different combinations can Richard order?

_____ combinations

Four girls shared an order of french fries. Monica had 2 times as many fries as Phoebe. Phoebe had 7 more fries than Rachel. Janice had half as many fries as Phoebe. Rachel had 9 fries. How many fries did each girl have?

Monica: _____

Phoebe: _____

Rachel: _____

Janice: _____

The answer is **a chocolate milkshake**. Write 3 different questions.

1. _____

2. _____

3. _____

The answer is **ketchup**. Write 3 different questions.

1. _____

2. _____

3. _____

Eating Out

The Jones family went out for dinner. Each person ordered something different. Read the clues and fill in the chart to find out what each person ordered. Make an X in a square when it __cannot__ be an answer. Draw a circle when it is a correct answer.

	Grandpa	Grandma	Dad	Mom	Josh	Becca
Hamburger						
Lasagna						
Fish and chips						
Baked salmon						
Spaghetti						
Chicken strips						

1. None of the males in the family ordered a dinner that contained pasta.

2. None of the adults ordered a hamburger.

3. The person who ordered spaghetti is younger than the person who ordered lasagna.

4. Dad is allergic to fish.

5. Grandma did __not__ order lasagna.

6. The person who ordered salmon shared some of it with his wife.

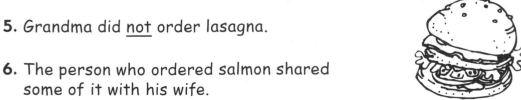

In the Car

Would you rather ride in the front seat or in the back seat? _____

Why? _____

_____

Use the clues to find the hidden joke and its answer.

- Cross off the names of things that can be found in or on a car.

- Cross off the words that are the names of fruits.

- Cross off the adverbs.

- Cross off the words that end in **L**.

WHAT	LEMON	DID	SOFTLY	BUMPER	REAL
WALL	THE	LIGHT	WIPER	GLADLY	CAR
SAY	RADIO	PEACH	TO	SEAT	APPLE
TIRE	THE	WELL	GRAPES	BRIDGE	?

YOU	LOUDLY	MAKE	GOAL	ME	CROSS

The Ingalls family drove from Seattle to Los Angeles in 2 days. The trip was 1,130 miles long. They drove 622 miles on the first day. How many miles did they drive on the second day?

_____ miles

Finish each sentence.

The car _____.

_____ that car _____.

_____ in the car.

 Critical and Creative Thinking Activities • EMC 3394 • © Evan-Moor Corp.

In the Car

Write 4 words to describe the last car that you rode in.

1. _____   3. _____

2. _____   4. _____

ANALOGIES

steering wheel : car :: handlebars : _____

convertible : car :: ferry : _____

headlights : two :: tires : _____

wipers : windshield :: horn : _____

Use the clues to complete each *car* word.

rug	car_____
vegetable	car_____
Mickey Mouse	car_____
to take somewhere	car_____
to shape with a knife	car_____
brown, chewy candy	car_____
cautious	car_____
rides and games	car_____
used to make boxes	car_____
animal that eats meat	car_____

How far does each vehicle go?

8   6   2   8

7   9

8   7

8   8   3   9

9

6   3   4   7

5

2

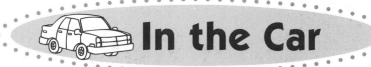

In the Car

Some people have special license plates with letters and numbers that create a short message. What do the license plates below say?

L8R G8R   DOUCME   LUV2SKI

_____ _____ _____

ICESK8R   IMHAPP   CR8TIV1

_____ _____ _____

ICU2   IML8   CCAPTN

_____ _____ _____

1GR8GAL   UR2SLO   CRAZ4U

_____ _____ _____

2CUTE4U   GR81   4U2NV

_____ _____ _____

On a Walk

Miles always takes the same path home from school. What are 3 reasons he might choose to walk home a different way?

1. _____

2. _____

3. _____

Think about the things that you might see on a walk in the country and in the city. Then fill in the chart. For each row, you must write words that begin with the letter you see on the left.

	In the Country	In the City
T		
C		
S		
F		
B		

Make each sentence more interesting by changing the verb and adding adjectives and adverbs.

The girl walked down the street.

_____

The man walked to the post office to mail the letter.

_____

On a Walk

Katie wants to walk to her friend's house, but she must get there alphabetically. Katie must step in order on each letter of the alphabet, starting at **A** and ending at **Z**. She may go up, down, sideways, or diagonally. Color Katie's path.

A	B	C	L	R	S	J	A	E	U	V	W	F	I
B	H	J	D	E	F	X	R	S	T	L	Y	X	B
C	D	B	T	M	G	Q	W	K	Q	U	G	Y	N
D	L	E	F	Y	A	K	P	P	R	L	V	X	O
E	B	M	G	D	J	W	D	O	S	V	W	A	P
A	F	T	W	H	I	E	A	N	T	U	X	B	C
C	G	B	E	I	C	D	M	B	J	P	A	Y	Z
P	E	H	A	J	K	L	M	N	O	X	B	C	D

• •

When Joe complained about having to walk to school, his father explained that when he was little, he had to walk 10 miles each way, uphill, and barefoot in the snow. Joe suspects that his father is exaggerating. Give 3 reasons why Joe might think this.

1. _____

2. _____

3. _____

Amanda and Olivia got new walking shoes. Olivia's shoes were two-and-a-half times more expensive than Amanda's shoes. Altogether, the shoes cost $91. How much did each girl's pair of shoes cost?

Amanda's shoes: $_____

Olivia's shoes: $_____

Emily can walk $3\frac{1}{2}$ miles in 1 hour. How many miles can she walk in 4 hours?

_____ miles

On a Walk

Four children walked to the park. Each child followed a different set of directions. Color each child's path with a different color.

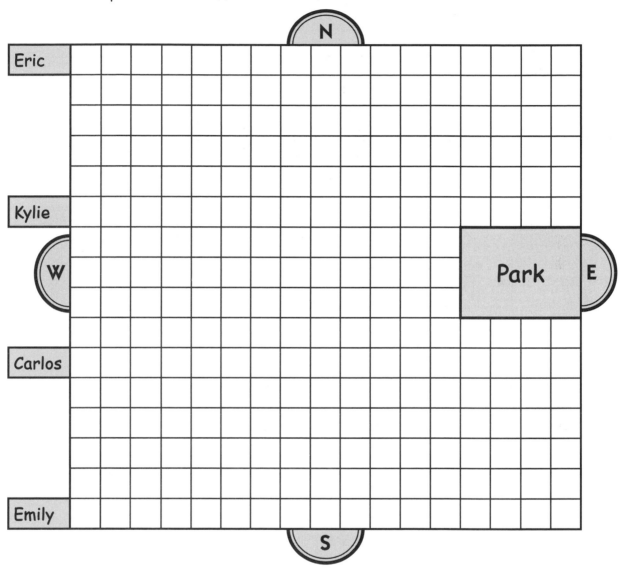

Eric	Kylie	Carlos	Emily
5 blocks East	2 blocks East	1 block East	9 blocks East
3 blocks South	2 blocks North	4 blocks South	4 blocks North
6 blocks East	2 blocks East	2 blocks East	2 blocks East
2 blocks North	5 blocks South	2 blocks North	3 blocks South
4 blocks East	4 blocks East	3 blocks East	6 blocks East
4 blocks South	3 blocks North	2 blocks North	3 blocks North
	3 blocks East	8 blocks East	2 blocks West
	1 block South	1 block North	2 blocks North
	2 blocks East		

At the Library

The answer is **at the library**. What is the question?

_____

The answer is **an overdue book**. What is the question?

_____

You want to check out a book about frogs. Number the steps from 1 to 9.

_____ Find the nonfiction section of the library.

_____ Choose the book you want.

_____ Write down the call number.

_____ Check out the book.

_____ Find the correct call number on the shelf.

_____ Go home and read the book.

_____ Go to the library.

_____ Look briefly at the different books about frogs.

_____ Look up the call number for books about frogs on the library computer.

Katie picked out a big stack of books. She looked through the stack and put half the books back. She checked out the remaining books and then gave one-third of them to her sister to read. That left Katie with 6 books. How many books did Katie originally have in her stack at the library?

_____ books

Conner was reading a library book when he discovered that pages 59 through 74 were missing! How many pieces of paper were missing from his book?

_____ pieces of paper

About how many times do you go to the library in a year? _____

Name _____

At the Library

Fill in the Venn diagram with at least 3 things in each section.

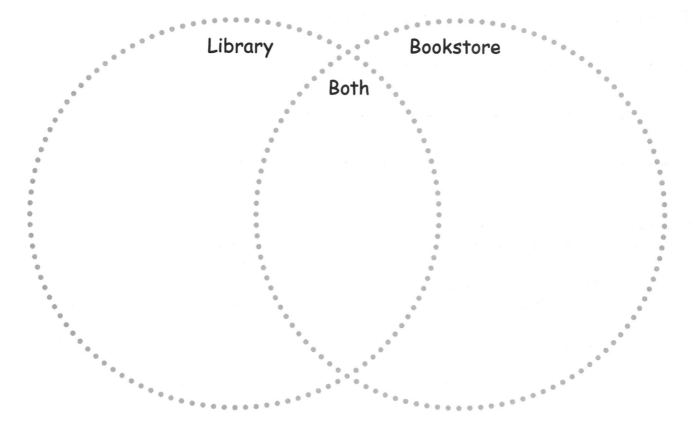

Library   Bookstore

Both

There are some things you can't do at the library. Why can't you...

talk loudly? _____

eat? _____

run? _____

take books without checking them out? _____

Alan checked out 23 books from the library. He returned them 6 days late. The fine is 10¢ a day per book. How much will Alan need to pay?	Alan paid his fine with a twenty-dollar bill. How much change will he get back?
$_____	$_____

Name _____

At the Library

The library books below were all written by authors with names that go with what they wrote about. Use the numbers to match the books with their authors.

1. How to Pay Off Your Debts

2. Karaoke for Everyone!

3. FINDING BURIED TREASURE

4. INTO THE HAUNTED HOUSE

5. Run Your Own Gas Station

6. Celebrity Lives

7. CLIMBING MOUNT EVEREST

8. At the Library

9. Fix Your Roof

10. First Aid for Beginners

11. Goodbye, My Love

12. Come Inside

_____ Lee King	_____ Owen Kash	_____ Hugo Furst
_____ Carrie A. Toon	_____ C.U. Later	_____ Doug A. Whole
_____ Phil R. Up	_____ Justin Case	_____ Rita Book
_____ Will E. Maykit	_____ Doris Open	_____ Rich N. Famous

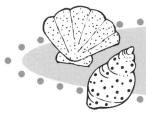

At the Beach

What is your favorite thing to do at the beach?

_____

What would be a silly thing to do at the beach?

_____

What can you find at the beach that begins with each letter?

S_____

T_____

W_____

D_____

C_____

You are going to the beach. What are the 4 most important things to take with you?

1. _____

2. _____

3. _____

4. _____

The answer is **at the beach.** What is the question?

_____

The answer is **a really big wave.** What is the question?

_____

What do they say?

c c c c c c c c c cc c c c c c c cccc c c c ccc ccc _____	Lifeguard ——————— Duty _____	**TIDE** _____

Name _____

At the Beach

Write a sentence that is always true about the beach.

_____

Write a sentence that is sometimes true about the beach.

_____

Write a sentence that is never true about the beach.

_____

Pamela went to the beach. She swam in the water before she ate lunch. She ate lunch before she made a sand castle. She made a sand castle after she got ice cream. Write what Pamela did in the correct order.

First: _____

Second: _____

Third: _____

Fourth: _____

There is a lot of sand at the beach! Number the places where you might find sand from 1 to 6. The worst place should be number 1.

_____ in your sandwich

_____ on your towel

_____ under your swimsuit

_____ in your hair

_____ on your ice cream

_____ in your eyes

Add 2 more words to the list, and then tell how the words are all related.

sea star, crab, clam, _____, _____

_____

towel, bucket, sunscreen, _____, _____

_____

Critical and Creative Thinking Activities • EMC 3394 • © Evan-Moor Corp.

At the Beach

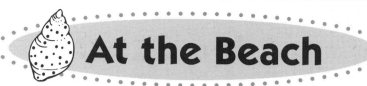

Joel, Maggie, Ramon, Shelly, and Adam each have a favorite activity they like to do at the beach. Read the clues and fill in the chart to find each child's favorite activity. Make an **X** in a square when it <u>cannot</u> be an answer. Draw a circle when it is a correct answer.

	Joel	Maggie	Ramon	Shelly	Adam
Building sand castles					
Swimming					
Looking for shells					
Playing volleyball					
Sunbathing					

1. Joel is afraid of the water.

2. Ramon and Adam do <u>not</u> like to play volleyball.

3. Maggie does <u>not</u> like to build sand castles.

4. None of the boys likes to look for shells.

5. Shelly loves to sunbathe.

6. Adam does <u>not</u> like to swim.

Name _____

On a Field Trip

If you could plan a field trip for your class, where would you go? _____

Why? _____

_____

Pilar's class went on a field trip to the aquarium. It took 42 minutes to get there on the bus. It took 9 minutes to get everyone organized once they got there. They looked at fish for 67 minutes, and then they had lunch for 38 minutes. After lunch, they watched the seals eat for 13 minutes, and then they went to a special presentation about tide pools for 45 minutes. It took 8 minutes to load the bus, and the ride back to school took 48 minutes. The class left the school at 9:00 a.m. At what time did they return?

_____

On the bus ride to the aquarium, James, Tim, Derek, Tonya, Jessica, and Dina sat in certain seats. Read the clues, and then write the children's names on their seats.

• Children with names that begin with the same letter sat together.

• The boys sat on the left.

• The children sat in alphabetical order, front to back.

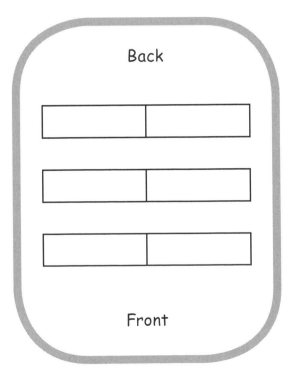

Critical and Creative Thinking Activities • EMC 3394 • © Evan-Moor Corp.

On a Field Trip

What are 3 things that you should <u>never</u> do on a field trip?

1. _____

2. _____

3. _____

The names of some places a class might go on a field trip are listed below. Number them from 1 to 6 according to how much you would like *going on* each trip.

_____ a science museum

_____ to see a play

_____ an art museum

_____ the aquarium

_____ the zoo

_____ a tour of a candy factory

• • • • • • • •

Everyone has to turn in a permission slip to go on the field trip. On Monday, half the class turned in their slips. On Tuesday, 9 more students turned in their slips. There are 28 students in the class. How many students have not yet turned in their slips?

_____ students

Find the answer to each clue by using the letters in these words:

FIELD TRIP

inside a peach _____

sleepy _____

to lose weight _____

group of lions _____

fib _____

scarlet _____

dessert _____

heap _____

turn over _____

ran away _____

for fingernails _____

On a Field Trip

Ryan has gotten separated from his class on the field trip. He needs to make it back to the bus before it leaves. To help Ryan get back to the bus, start at the square in the upper-left corner. Move the same number of squares as the number shown (2). Move in a straight line in any direction. When you get to the next square, move the same number of squares as the number shown. Can you make a path that will take Ryan to the bus? Color the path.

②	7	3	6	1	5	9	2	1	8	4	3
5	2	2	6	3	1	3	7	5	2	9	1
7	8	1	6	2	7	1	5	2	6	6	2
1	3	4	2	7	2	4	4	7	1	1	7
2	7	3	6	1	3	9	2	1	8	4	3
1	3	4	2	7	2	4	4	7	2	1	7
5	2	2	6	3	1	3	7	5	2	9	1
7	8	1	6	2	4	3	2	2	4	6	2
2	7	3	6	1	4	9	2	1	2	4	6
1	3	4	2	7	2	3	8	3	2	1	2
7	8	1	6	2	1	1	4	2	6	6	1
5	2	2	8	3	1	3	5	3	2	3	1

6-Legged Crawlies

Would you rather be an ant, a cricket, or a ladybug? _____

Why? _____

_____

What kind of insect does this fact describe?

Fact: The biggest kinds of these insects live in Costa Rica. Their wingspans can be as long as 7½ inches!

To find the name of this insect, first circle the names of 12 different insects in the word search. Next, write the remaining letters on the lines. Then unscramble the letters to name the insect.

Letters: ____ ____ ____ ____ ____ ____ ____ ____ ____ ____

The hidden insect is a _____.

```
M  O  S  Q  U  I  T  O
T  T  F  L  Y  C  L  B
E  E  G  I  W  R  A  E
R  N  R  F  A  I  D  E
M  R  G  N  S  C  Y  T
I  O  T  Y  P  K  B  L
T  H  T  D  O  E  U  E
E  N  A  H  L  T  G
```

How many flies are there?

_____ in only the circle

_____ in only the rectangle

_____ in only the rectangle and circle

_____ in only the triangle and circle

_____ in only the rectangle and triangle

_____ in all 3 shapes

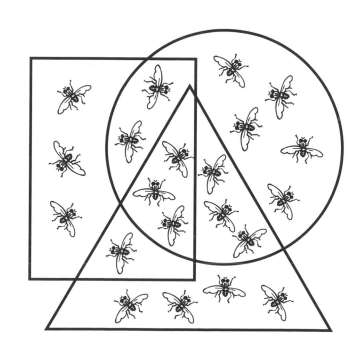

Name _____

6-Legged Crawlies

Are you afraid of bugs? _____ Why or why not? _____

_____

Fill in the missing vowels.

___ N T

M ___ T H

C R ___ C K ___ T

H ___ ___ S ___ F L Y

L ___ D Y B ___ G

B ___ ___ T L ___

G R ___ S S H ___ P P ___ R

M ___ S Q ___ ___ T ___

P R ___ Y ___ N G   M ___ N T ___ S

S T ___ N K   B ___ G

C ___ C K R ___ ___ C H

Tamara was catching ladybugs to put in her garden. She caught 17 ladybugs on Wednesday. She caught a total of 33 ladybugs on Thursday and Friday. She caught a total of 41 ladybugs on Wednesday and Thursday. How many ladybugs did Tamara catch on each day?

Wednesday: _____

Thursday: _____

Friday: _____

How many bugs did she catch on all 3 days?

_____

ANALOGIES

beetle : insect :: lizard : _____

cricket : green :: ladybug : _____

ant : hill :: bee : _____

insect : six :: spider : _____

Critical and Creative Thinking Activities • EMC 3394 • © Evan-Moor Corp.

6-Legged Crawlies

Look at each pattern of bugs in the box at the top of the page. Then find the same pattern in the grid below and color it. Use a different color for each pattern.

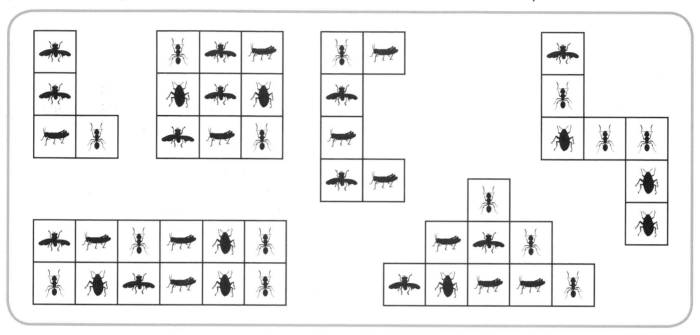

Name _____

Big Birds

How are an ostrich and a flamingo the same and how are they different? Think of 3 ways for each.

Same	Different

Add adjectives and adverbs to make the sentence more interesting.

The eagle flew over the meadow.

_____

Fill in the missing vowels to name the birds. Then find them in the word search.

ST __ R K

__ S T R __ C H

__ __ G L __

P __ L __ C __ N

T __ R K __ Y

H __ R __ N

V __ L T __ R __

F L __ M __ N G __

```
T  N  E  E  I  N  E  O  T  I
O  G  N  I  M  A  L  F  S  P
S  T  P  V  O  C  G  I  K  G
T  I  R  O  U  I  A  E  N  T
R  G  K  O  H  L  E  R  E  T
I  U  R  V  L  E  T  Y  C  U
C  O  T  I  O  P  R  U  O  R
H  E  E  O  S  S  T  O  R  K
R  R  P  T  A  U  L  K  N  E
P  R  H  N  A  U  F  E  A  Y
```

Critical and Creative Thinking Activities • EMC 3394 • © Evan-Moor Corp.

Big Birds

The bald eagle is a symbol of the United States, but Benjamin Franklin had wanted the wild turkey to be the symbol. Do you think Franklin's idea was good or bad? _____

Give 3 reasons to support your opinion.

1. _____

2. _____

3. _____

An ostrich can run half a mile in a minute. How long will it take each of the ostriches below to run to the water hole?

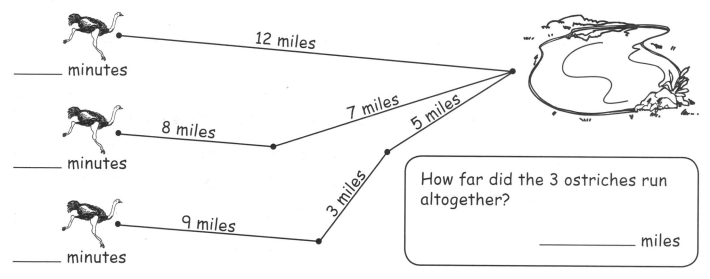

_____ minutes   12 miles

_____ minutes   8 miles   7 miles   5 miles

_____ minutes   9 miles   3 miles

How far did the 3 ostriches run altogether?

_____ miles

What does it mean to be "as proud as a peacock"?

_____

Why do people use a peacock for this expression instead of another kind of bird?

_____

Name _____

Big Birds

The ostrich is the world's biggest bird, but is it worth the most points? Use the number chart to find out. For each bird listed below, find the number of points for each letter and write it on the line. Then add the numbers to find out how much that bird is worth.

A	B	C	D	E	F	G	H	I	J	K	L	M
1	2	3	4	5	6	7	8	9	10	11	12	13
N	O	P	Q	R	S	T	U	V	W	X	Y	Z
14	15	16	17	18	19	20	21	22	23	24	25	26

O   S   T   R   I   C   H

15   19   ___ ___ ___ ___ ___ = ___

C   O   N   D   O   R

___ ___ ___ ___ ___ ___ = ___

T   U   R   K   E   Y

___ ___ ___ ___ ___ ___ = ___

V   U   L   T   U   R   E

___ ___ ___ ___ ___ ___ ___ = ___

F   L   A   M   I   N   G   O

___ ___ ___ ___ ___ ___ ___ ___ = ___

> Which bird is worth the least points?
>
> _____
>
> Which bird is worth the most points?
>
> _____

40 Critical and Creative Thinking Activities • EMC 3394 • © Evan-Moor Corp.

Name _____

Wild Cats

Write something that is true about tigers but <u>not</u> true about panthers.

_____

Write something that is true about leopards but <u>not</u> true about lions.

_____

Unscramble the letters to find the names of big cats. Then write the words in the grid.

RITGE _____

GUCARO _____

COBBAT _____

ONIL _____

GURAJA _____

AHECTEH _____

PEDRALO _____

NEPARHT _____

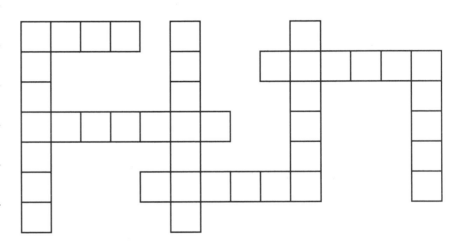

Carson went to a wildlife park. He saw tigers before he saw lions. He saw cheetahs after he saw jaguars. He saw cheetahs before tigers. In what order did Carson see the 4 kinds of cats?

First: _____

Second: _____

Third: _____

Fourth: _____

Wild Cats

What does it mean to get the "lion's share" of something?

_____

What is something that you would like to have the lion's share of?

_____

The Happytown Zoo has fewer cheetahs than it has lions.
It has more jaguars than it has cheetahs.

Write **T** if the statement is **true**.
Write **F** if the statement is **false**.
Write **C** if you **can't be sure**.

_____ There are more lions than cheetahs.

_____ There are fewer jaguars than cheetahs.

_____ There are fewer jaguars than lions.

_____ There are more jaguars than lions.

_____ There are more cheetahs than lions.

Finish the tongue twisters.

Leo Lion loves _____

Tia the Tiger tried _____

Carl Cougar could _____

Immediately behind one of these doors, there is a hungry tiger that will eat you. Behind the other door is a big bag of candy that you can eat. You <u>must</u> open one door. To help you decide, read the signs on the doors. Only one of them is a true statement. The candy is behind the door with the true statement. Circle the door you decide to open.

There is a tiger behind the other door and candy behind this door.

There is a tiger behind one door and candy behind the other door.

Critical and Creative Thinking Activities • EMC 3394 • © Evan-Moor Corp.

Name _____

Wild Cats

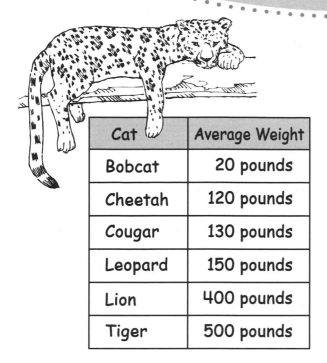

Cat	Average Weight
Bobcat	20 pounds
Cheetah	120 pounds
Cougar	130 pounds
Leopard	150 pounds
Lion	400 pounds
Tiger	500 pounds

Use the chart to answer the questions.

If you had one each of the big cats listed, how much would they weigh altogether?

_____ pounds

How much heavier is a lion than a cheetah?

_____ pounds

How much heavier is a tiger than a cougar?

_____ pounds

How much heavier is a leopard than a bobcat?

_____ pounds

Imagine that you have a scale. Your job is to make the scale balanced.

There is a lion on one side. Which 3 cats do you put on the other side?

_____, _____, _____

There are 2 tigers on one side. You put several of the same kind of cat on the other side.

Kind of cat: _____ How many: _____

Which 3 cats weigh 300 pounds altogether?

_____, _____, _____

Which is heavier? Circle it.

5 cheetahs or 1 tiger

7 leopards or 2 tigers

12 bobcats or 2 cougars

4 cougars or 3 leopards

2 lions or 5 leopards

6 cheetahs or 5 leopards

3 tigers or 5 lions

Sssssnakes

In Greek mythology, Medusa had live snakes for hair! List 5 problems that someone with snake-hair would have. Then draw a portrait of Medusa.

1. _____

_____

2. _____

_____

3. _____

_____

4. _____

_____

5. _____

_____

MEDUSA

176 anacondas decided to line up end to end. The anacondas were all the same length. Altogether, the line of anacondas was a mile long (5,280 feet). How long was each anaconda?

_____ feet long

Write 4 adjectives that begin with **S** to describe snakes.

S_____

S_____

S_____

S_____

Name _____

Ssssnakes

There are nearly 3,000 kinds of snakes. How many kinds can you name?

1. _____   5. _____

2. _____   6. _____

3. _____   7. _____

4. _____   8. _____

Sally Snake is longer than **Susie Snake**. **Sammy Snake** is longer than **Sally Snake**. **Simon Snake** is shorter than **Susie Snake**. Put the 4 snakes in order from longest to shortest.

_____

_____

_____

_____

Jake the Snake is a yard and a foot plus an inch long. How long is Jake the Snake in inches?

_____ inches long

Blake the Snake is one-eighth of two yards long. How many inches long is Blake the Snake?

_____ inches long

Compose a short rhyming poem using the words *snake*, *bake*, *cake*, and *lake*.

_____

_____

_____

_____

_____

Illustrate your poem.

Ssssnakes

Follow the directions to find a fact about snakes. Then write the fact on the line.

Cross out these letters: **R, M, J, B, U, C, Z**

SMNJRABCKUEMSDCOUNUOZTRHBARVEEYZJUELJICDSR

_____

Cross out 5 foods.

SNSOUPAKESSMCAKEELLWIAPPLETHTBEANHEIRTOPIENGUES

_____

Cross out 5 colors.

SNAREDKESEBLUEATTHBLACKEIRPREPINKYWHOWHITELE

_____

Cross out 9 three-letter words.

SCATNSITALOWKJAMESDOGARUNRYESEDEPITAKITF

_____

Critical and Creative Thinking Activities • EMC 3394 • © Evan-Moor Corp.

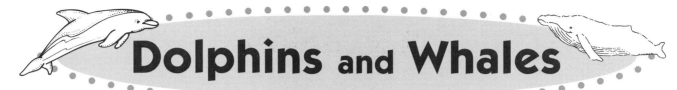

Dolphins and Whales

The answer is **a blue whale**. What is the question?

_____

The answer is **a playful dolphin**. What is the question?

_____

Use the words *DOLPHINS* and *WHALES* to make new 4-letter words. You must use 2 letters from each word.
Example: *nose*

_____   _____

_____   _____

_____   _____

Add a whale to this picture.

What does the largest animal in the world eat? Cross out the letters in the names of things that a blue whale does <u>not</u> eat to find out what it <u>does</u> eat.

N D A S K O R S A T R U R A I E O S W E S E L O S E L P C E T S P

- A blue whale does <u>not</u> eat SEAWEED.

- A blue whale does <u>not</u> eat SEA STARS.

- A blue whale would <u>not</u> eat an OCTOPUS.

- A blue whale would <u>not</u> eat a PERSON.

A blue whale eats _____.

(about 40 million a day!)

Dolphins and Whales

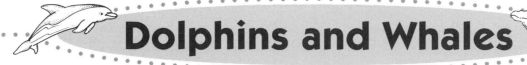

Fill in the Venn diagram with at least 3 things in each section.

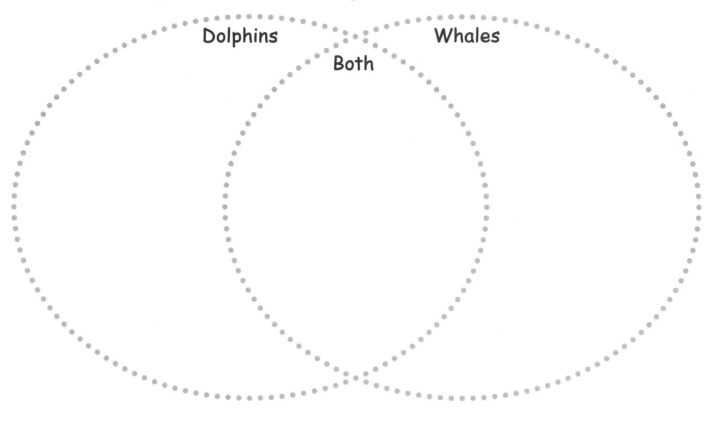

Dolphins

Both

Whales

Danny Dolphin likes to eat fish. Yesterday, he ate 7 mackerels, 23 herrings, and 42 sardines. How many fish did Danny eat altogether?

_____ fish

Today, Danny ate 78 fish. He ate the same number of mackerels as yesterday. He ate 31 herrings. How many sardines did Danny eat today?

_____ sardines

Dora Dolphin is bigger than Danny Dolphin. Donna Dolphin is smaller than Dora Dolphin.

Write **T** if the statement is **true**, **F** if the statement is **false**, and **C** if you **can't be sure**.

_____ Dora is bigger than Danny and Donna.

_____ Donna is smaller than Danny.

_____ Donna and Danny are the same size.

_____ Danny is bigger than Dora.

_____ Dora is the biggest dolphin.

_____ Danny and Donna are twins.

Dolphins and Whales

Use the chart to make a bar graph showing the approximate length of each kind of whale. Use different colors to help the bars stand out.

Whale	Average Length
Humpback	45 feet
Orca	25 feet
Gray	40 feet
Blue	90 feet
Fin	80 feet
Minke	30 feet
Sperm	55 feet
Pilot	20 feet
Northern Right	50 feet

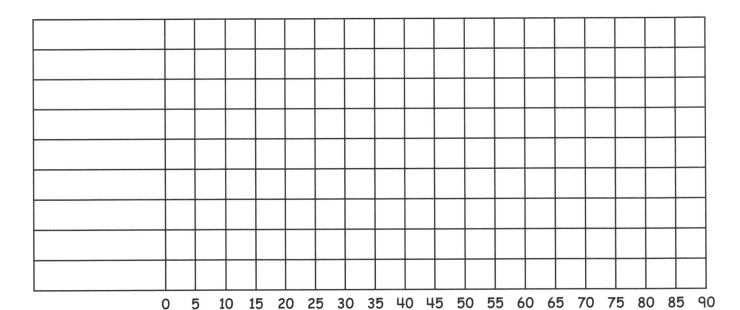

0 5 10 15 20 25 30 35 40 45 50 55 60 65 70 75 80 85 90

Use information from your bar graph to write a sentence about whales.

_____

_____

_____

Name _____

Trees

Write 3 things that all trees have in common.

1. _____

2. _____

3. _____

The tree names below are missing their vowels. Fill in the letters, and then write the names of the trees in the grid.

___ L M   D ___ G W ___ ___ D

F ___ R   H ___ M L ___ C K

___ ___ K   R ___ D W ___ ___ D

P ___ L M

P ___ N ___

B ___ ___ C H

B ___ R C H

C ___ D ___ R

M ___ P L ___

W ___ L L ___ W

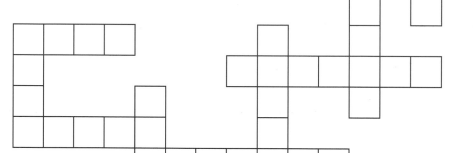

Write a sentence about a tree. Use exactly 8 words.

_____

Name _____

 **Trees**

Many kinds of animals live in trees. How many kinds can you think of?

_____   _____   _____

_____   _____   _____

_____   _____   _____

ANALOGIES

tree : bark :: person : _____

pine : tree :: beagle : _____

acorn : oak :: cone : _____

apple : tree :: berry : _____

Would you like to live in a treehouse? _____

Why or why not? _____

_____

Emily and Penelope were picking apples. Emily picked 3 times more apples than Penelope. Altogether, they picked 168 apples. How many apples did each girl pick?

Emily: _____

Penelope: _____

There are 7 trees in a row. Each tree is 1½ feet taller than the tree before it. The first tree is 22 feet tall. How tall is the last tree?

_____ feet tall

Name _____

Trees

Can you decode this joke about trees?

A	B	C	D	E	F	G	H	I	J	K	L	M
Z	Y	X	W	V	U	T	S	R	Q	P	O	N

N	O	P	Q	R	S	T	U	V	W	X	Y	Z
M	L	K	J	I	H	G	F	E	D	C	B	A

D S Z G W R W G S V

___ ___ ___ ___ ___ ___ ___ ___ ___ ___

G I V V D V Z I G L

___ ___ ___ ___ ___ ___ ___ ___ ___ ___

G S V H D R N N R M T

___ ___ ___ ___ ___ ___ ___ ___ ___ ___ ___

K Z I G B

___ ___ ___ ___ ___ ?

Answer:

H D R N G I F M P H

___ ___ ___ ___ ___ ___ ___ ___ ___ ___ !

Mountains

Draw It:

There are 2 mountains.

The one on the left is a little bigger than the one on the right.

There is snow on top of both of them.

The sun is rising between them.

Mount Everest is the tallest mountain in the world. What other mountains can you name?

_____   _____

_____   _____

_____   _____

Mount Everest is 29,035 feet tall. How tall is Mount Everest rounded to the nearest…

ten? _____

hundred? _____

thousand? _____

ten thousand? _____

Write the numbers 1–6 in the circles so that the sum of all 3 sides is 9. Use each number only once.

Mountains

Write a sentence that is always true about mountains.

_____

Write a sentence that is sometimes true about mountains.

_____

Write a sentence that is never true about mountains.

_____

Make a mountain of words. Use the letters in the word *mountains* to make as many smaller words as you can.

MOUNTAINS

_____   _____

_____   _____   _____

_____   _____   _____

_____   _____   _____

What does it mean to "make a mountain out of a molehill"?

_____

Write an example of someone making a mountain out of a molehill.

_____

_____

Name _____

Mountains

How tall are the 6 tallest mountains in the United States? Use the clues to find out how tall each mountain is. Make an **X** in a square when it <u>cannot</u> be an answer. Draw a circle when it is a correct answer.

		Elevations					
		20,320 feet	14,505 feet	14,440 feet	14,410 feet	13,804 feet	13,796 feet
Mountains	**Mount Rainier** Washington						
	Gannett Peak Wyoming						
	Mount Elbert Colorado						
	Mauna Kea Hawaii						
	Mount McKinley Alaska						
	Mount Whitney California						

1. The 2 mountains that are in states that begin with **C** are over 14,000 feet tall. Neither one is the tallest mountain.

2. The tallest and the smallest mountains are located in Hawaii or Alaska.

3. Gannett Peak is under 14,000 feet tall.

4. Mount Elbert is taller than Mount Rainier but not as tall as Mount Whitney.

5. The mountain in Wyoming is just 8 feet taller than Mauna Kea.

Name _____

Caught in a Storm

How many different kinds of storms can you name?

_____   _____

_____   _____

_____   _____

You know you will be caught in a storm. You can have <u>only</u> one of the things listed below. Circle the one you choose.

raincoat   rain poncho

umbrella   sunglasses

rain boots   rain hat

Why? _____

_____

_____

How many inches of snow fell during the big storm?

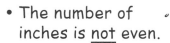

- It snowed more than 2 feet but less than 3 feet.

- The number of inches is <u>not</u> even.

- If you add the digits of the number together, the sum is 11.

_____ inches of snow fell.

What do they say?

STOcaught**RM**	**WINDS**	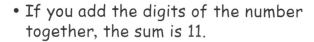 storm storm storm storm storm storm storm storm storm storm storm storm storm storm storm storm storm
_____	_____	_____

    Critical and Creative Thinking Activities • EMC 3394 • © Evan-Moor Corp.

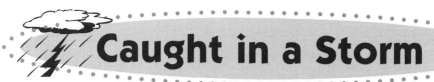

Caught in a Storm

You and a friend are hiking and you get caught in a snowstorm. Luckily, you have warm jackets in your daypacks. What are 3 things that you can do to help you survive until help comes?

1. _____

2. _____

3. _____

Unscramble the storm-related words. Then find them in the word search. Use the remaining letters in the word search to make the name of a U.S. city that suffered a major hurricane in August 2005.

LIHA _____

DWIN _____

WOSN _____

NIRA _____

SETLE _____

TEEWHAR _____

SOLDUC _____

DREHUNT _____

ZADRIBZL _____

DOONTAR _____

GGIINNHLT _____

L	I	G	H	T	N	I	N	G
W			W	H	S	W	C	T
E			S	U	I	O	L	E
A	T	O	R	N	A	D	O	E
T	E	N	D	D	O	L	U	L
H	A	I	L	E	A	W	D	S
E	N	I	A	R	R	N	S	E
R	D	R	A	Z	Z	I	L	B

Remaining letters:

__ __ __ __ __ __ __ __ __ __ __

The city that suffered a major hurricane is

_____ _____.

Caught in a Storm

Each year, the United States National Weather Service gives names to hurricanes. The name of the first hurricane of the year begins with **A**, the second with **B**, the third with **C**, and so on, through the letter **W**. The letters **Q** and **U** are <u>not</u> used.

The National Weather Service has 6 lists of hurricane names that they rotate every 6 years. The names of hurricanes that cause a lot of damage, like Hurricane Katrina, are retired. When a name is retired, a new name must be added. Your job is to make a new list of names that could be used when a name is retired. Try to think of a name for each letter.

A_____   L_____

B_____   M_____

C_____   N_____

D_____   O_____

E_____   P_____

F_____   R_____

G_____   S_____

H_____   T_____

I_____   V_____

J_____   W_____

K_____

Why do you think people give names to hurricanes?

_____

_____

_____

Fictional Characters

Name _____

Who was the last fictional character you read about? _____

What book is he or she from? _____

Write 3 words to describe the character.

_____   _____   _____

Do you like the character? _____ Why or why not? _____

_____

Name a fictional character who fits each adjective. Try to think of a different character for each word.

kind _____

bossy _____

smart _____

brave _____

mean _____

silly _____

shy _____

dishonest _____

dependable _____

lazy _____

I am big and green. My name begins with S. Who am I?

_____

I made friends with 7 little people. I like apples. Who am I?

_____

I live in the ocean. I wear a tie. I am yellow. Who am I?

_____

I am orange and white. I can swim. I got lost. Who am I?

_____

I wear a big red and white striped hat. I talk in rhymes. Who am I?

_____

Fictional Characters

ANALOGIES

Shiloh : dog :: Charlotte : _____

Charlie Bucket : Roald Dahl :: Harry Potter : _____

Jack Spratt : nursery rhyme :: Cinderella : _____

You are having a party and can invite any 6 fictional characters. Fill in the chart to show who you invite, where they come from, and why you invited them. You will want your guests to get along and have a good time, so plan carefully.

Character	Book/Movie/TV Show	Why

An Oompa-Loompa can make 258 Everlasting Gobstoppers in one hour. How many can he make in 36 hours?

_____ Everlasting Gobstoppers

Peter Pan lives in Neverland, so he never grows up. If Peter was 9 years old when he got to Neverland in 1911 (when the book was published), how many years old would he be today?

_____ years old

Name _____

Fictional Characters

Fill in the chart to show what you think are each character's favorites. For the last two, fill in the characters of your choice. Use your imagination!

Character	Favorite Food	Favorite Place	Favorite Color	Hobby
Willy Wonka				
The Big Bad Wolf				
Curious George				
Peter Pan				
Wilbur (the pig)				
Snow White				
Mickey Mouse				
Donkey (from *Shrek*)				

Which character would make the best friend? _____

Why do you think so? _____

_____

Friends

What are 6 traits of a good friend?

1. _____   4. _____

2. _____   5. _____

3. _____   6. _____

Do you think you are a good friend? _____

Why or why not? _____

_____

Grace asked 27 of her friends what they like on their ice cream. 19 of them like hot fudge. 16 of them like whipped cream. 9 of them like both hot fudge and whipped cream. How many of Grace's friends do not like hot fudge or whipped cream?

_____ friend(s)

Ben and his dad went hiking with 6 friends. They left at 9:30 in the morning. They hiked 7 miles. They saw 6 squirrels, 3 deer, and 7 rabbits. Including a stop for lunch, the hike lasted for $5\frac{1}{2}$ hours. They drank 9 bottles of water. At what time did they finish the hike?

_____

How many people were on the hike?

_____ people

Write a sentence using the words *friend*, *play*, *game*, and *toothbrush*.

_____

_____

 Critical and Creative Thinking Activities • EMC 3394 • © Evan-Moor Corp.

Name _____

Friends

What is the difference between a friend and an acquaintance?

_____

Would you rather have a lot of acquaintances or just one good friend? _____

Why? _____

Maria invited 17 friends to her birthday party. 13 of her friends are from school. 9 of her friends are from her soccer team. How many of Maria's friends are kids she knows from school who are also on her soccer team?

_____ friends

Desmond wants to share the cookies in his lunch with his 2 best friends. Draw lines to show how he can divide them so all 3 boys get an equal amount.

5 friends went to the movies. Juliet sat next to Ben. Charlie sat between Claire and Hugo. Ben sat farthest to the left. The two girls sat next to each other. Write the children's names in the order they sat.

_____   _____   _____   _____   _____

Who have you been friends with the longest? _____

Who is your newest friend? _____

What do you think this expression means?

"Make new friends, but keep the old. One is silver and the other gold."

_____

Name _____

Friends

These children are all friends. Each child has made a list of 3 favorite activities. Today, each child gets to do one of his or her favorite activities with a friend. For each activity listed at the bottom of the page, write the names of 2 children on the lines next to it. The activity must appear on each child's list of favorites, and each child may do only one activity.

Mandy	**Matthew**	**Andy**	**Daniel**
Ice-skating	Video games	Ice-skating	Movies
Frisbee	Movies	Mini golf	Frisbee
Movies	Magic show	Baking cookies	Video games

Isabel	**Jacob**	**Hannah**	**Madison**
Movies	Mini golf	Frisbee	Riding bikes
Magic show	Video games	Baking cookies	Mini golf
Frisbee	Movies	Movies	Ice-skating

Michael	**Perry**	**Will**	**Abby**
Video games	Baking cookies	Video games	Riding bikes
Riding bikes	Ice-skating	Riding bikes	Movies
Baking cookies	Mini golf	Magic show	Mini golf

Sophie	**Elly**	**Ethan**	**Olivia**
Movies	Riding bikes	Frisbee	Magic show
Mini golf	Movies	Movies	Riding bikes
Ice-skating	Baking cookies	Ice-skating	Ice-skating

- Riding bikes _____ and _____

- Baking cookies _____ and _____

- Ice-skating _____ and _____

- Movies _____ and _____

- Mini golf _____ and _____

- Video games _____ and _____

- Magic show _____ and _____

- Frisbee _____ and _____

   Critical and Creative Thinking Activities • EMC 3394 • © Evan-Moor Corp.

Family Tree

Lester and Sadie had 4 children. Each of their children had 3 children. Each of those children had 2 children. How many great-grandchildren do Lester and Sadie have?

_____

Your mother's father is your _____.

Your father's sister is your _____.

Your grandmother's daughter is your _____.

Your uncle's child is your _____.

Your father's grandfather is your _____.

Your grandfather's sister is your _____.

Your sister's son would be your _____.

Being the oldest or the youngest or an only child has advantages and disadvantages. Fill in the chart to show at least one for each.

	Advantages	Disadvantages
Oldest		
Youngest		
Only child		

If you could choose, would you want to be the oldest, the youngest, or an only child?

_____ Why? _____

_____

Family Tree

How many people are in your immediate family?

_____

How many people are in your family, including grandparents, aunts, uncles, and cousins?

_____

You are a son or a daughter. What other family roles do you have?

_____

_____

_____

_____

Write 5 words to describe your father.

1. _____
2. _____
3. _____
4. _____
5. _____

How are you the same as your father?

_____

_____

How are you different from your father?

_____

_____

Write 5 words to describe your mother.

1. _____
2. _____
3. _____
4. _____
5. _____

How are you the same as your mother?

_____

_____

How are you different from your mother?

_____

_____

    Critical and Creative Thinking Activities • EMC 3394 • © Evan-Moor Corp.

Family Tree

Use the clues to fill in the names on the family tree. You will probably need to read the clues at least 2 times.

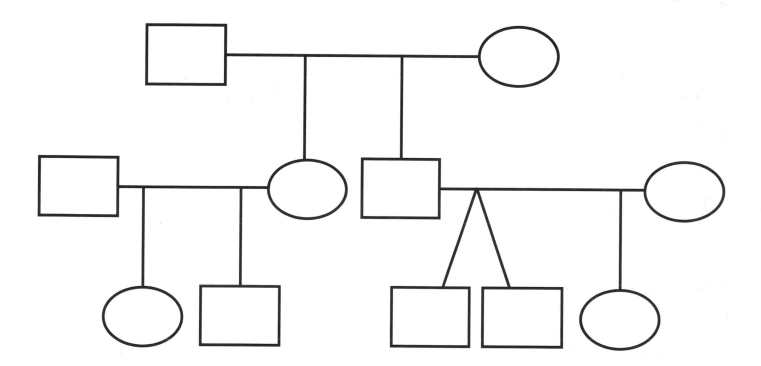

Male = ☐   Female = ◯   Married = ——   Child = |

Family Members

Micah	Rachel
Bob	Sasha
David	Sue
Scott	Lucy
Ethan	Fay
Shane	

- Rachel and Ethan are siblings.

- Lucy and David are siblings.

- Micah and Shane are twins.

- Sue is Lucy's grandma.

- Ethan is Sasha's father.

- Rachel is married to Scott.

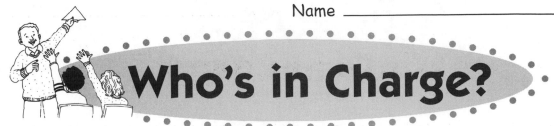

Who's in Charge?

Being in charge is not always easy! What are 3 things that a good leader does?

1. _____

2. _____

3. _____

What are 3 things that a bad leader does?

1. _____

2. _____

3. _____

When you are a child, adults are in charge. Who are some of the adults in charge of you?

_____ _____

_____ _____

_____ _____

Michael is in charge of Dwight. Jan is in charge of Michael. Dwight is in charge of Pam. Write **T** if the statement is **true**. Write **F** if the statement is **false**.

_____ Michael is in charge of everyone.

_____ Pam is in charge of no one.

_____ Jan is in charge of everyone.

Your teacher is in charge of your class. If you could change one thing about the way she or he manages the classroom, what would it be?

_____

_____

_____

Name _____

Who's in Charge?

If you were in charge of your class for the next 15 minutes, what would you do?

_____

_____

Adults are not always in charge. They often have bosses or supervisors where they work. Who is in charge of the people listed below?

Teacher _____

Grocery checker _____

Football player _____

Actor _____

Firefighter _____

Dental assistant _____

Deputy _____

Author _____

Carla is the president of a computer software company. She has 7 vice presidents. Each vice president has 4 managers. Each manager has 14 programmers.

How many programmers work for Carla's company?

_____ programmers

How many people (including Carla) work at Carla's company altogether?

_____ people

Who is in charge of the president of the United States? _____

Why do you think so?

_____

_____

_____

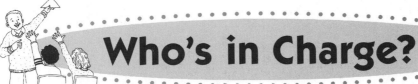

Who's in Charge?

Who owns the businesses listed below? Use the clues to find out. Make an **X** in a square when it <u>cannot</u> be an answer. Draw a circle when it is a correct answer.

	Business Owners					
Businesses	Mr. Appleton	Ms. Billings	Mr. Carlson	Mrs. Deets	Mr. Everett	Ms. Ford
Toilet Town						
Wrench Warehouse						
Mostly Mittens						
Paper Clip Palace						
Exclusively Eggs						
The Fork Factory						

1. Mr. Carlson and Mrs. Deets do <u>not</u> own businesses that sell things that are made from metal.

2. Ms. Billings is dating the man who sells toilets. Her best friend is the woman who manufactures mittens.

3. Mr. Appleton does <u>not</u> sell paper clips or toilets.

4. The person who sells forks has been considering expanding her business to include spoons. But when she talked to Ms. Ford about it, Ms. Ford did not think it was such a good idea.

5. In order to get a jump on the competition, Mr. Carlson sells his product in a carton of 13 instead of the usual dozen.

Name _____

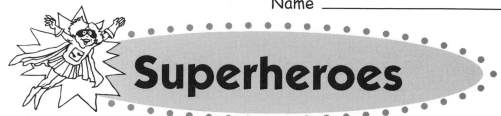

Superheroes

How many superheroes can you name? Use the back if you need more room.

1. _____   5. _____

2. _____   6. _____

3. _____   7. _____

4. _____   8. _____

Number the superpowers from 1 to 8. The one you think is best should be number 1.

_____ super strength

_____ invisibility

_____ flight

_____ shape shifting

_____ super speed

_____ X-ray vision

_____ weather control

_____ breathe underwater

Batman captured 11 bad guys on Tuesday. On Wednesday and Thursday, he captured a total of 23 bad guys. He captured a total of 18 bad guys on Tuesday and Wednesday. How many bad guys did Batman capture on each day?

Tuesday: _____

Wednesday: _____

Thursday: _____

How many bad guys did Batman capture altogether?

_____ bad guys

Write a sentence about a superhero. Use exactly 3 words.

_____

Write a sentence about a superhero. Use exactly 10 words.

_____

Name _____

Superheroes

If you could have one superpower, what would it be? _____

Why? _____

_____

ANALOGIES

Spiderman : red :: The Incredible Hulk : _____

Clark Kent : Superman :: Bruce Wayne : _____

Wonder Woman : invisible plane :: Batman : _____

How do you think our world might be different if superheroes really existed?

_____

_____

If superheroes did exist, would you want to be one? _____

Why or why not? _____

Superwoman has had a busy day. First, she flew 1,247 miles from her home in Metropolis to New York, where she saved a little girl from being run over by a taxi. Next, she sped 3,628 miles to Paris to keep an earthquake from tumbling the Eiffel Tower. After that, it was 8,493 miles to China, where she arrived just in time to catch a man who'd fallen off the Great Wall. Then she flew 4,586 miles to Australia to capture some escaped criminals. Finally, she flew 9,364 miles home to Metropolis. How many miles did Superwoman fly altogether?

_____ miles

Critical and Creative Thinking Activities • EMC 3394 • © Evan-Moor Corp.

Superheroes

Invent a superhero! First, answer the questions about your superhero. Then draw a picture of him or her. Your superhero can be serious or silly.

What is your superhero called?

_____

What superpowers does he or she have?

_____

_____

_____

_____

_____

_____

How did your superhero get his or her superpowers?

_____

_____

_____

What kinds of things does your superhero do to help people?

_____

_____

_____

Name _____

Elves and Fairies

Elves and fairies are often in storybooks. What stories have you read or had read to you that included these kinds of characters?

1. _____   4. _____

2. _____   5. _____

3. _____   6. _____

How do you think elves and fairies are the same?

_____

_____

How do you think elves and fairies are different?

_____

_____

Fairies love to frolic in the meadow. Yesterday, the fairies got up at dawn, which was at 5:43, and frolicked until dusk, which was at 9:24. How long did the fairies frolic?

_____ hours _____ minutes

Elves have been known to make shoes for people during the night. If an elf can make a pair of shoes in half an hour, how many pairs of shoes can 3 elves make in 8 hours?

_____ pairs of shoes

Would you like to be an elf? _____ Why or why not? _____

_____

 Critical and Creative Thinking Activities • EMC 3394 • © Evan-Moor Corp.

Elves and Fairies

Find the word for each clue. Each word is made from the letters in these 3 words:

ELVES AND FAIRIES

good with burgers _____

shirts have two _____

opposite of more _____

forest animal with hooves _____

not dead _____

sun does this early _____

water goes down this _____

land with water around it _____

not a captive _____

Draw an elf. Then write what you think the elf might say.

Fairies are thought to have magic.
What are 4 magical things that fairies might be able to do?

1. _____

2. _____

3. _____

4. _____

Fairy and *ferry* are homophones. Write a homophone for each word below.

flower _____   sun _____   merry _____

wood _____   root _____   reed _____

Name _____

Elves and Fairies

Can you find each fairy's favorite flower? The numbered flowers are at the bottom of the page. Read each clue, and then write the number of the flower in the circle. You will use each flower <u>only</u> once, so you may want to cross them out as you go.

Dew Drop
Both digits in my flower are odd. If you add them together, the sum is greater than 10.

Sprite
If you double the ones digit in my flower, you get the tens digit.

Thistle
Multiply a one-digit number by itself to get my flower.

Fern
My flower is one more than three dozen.

Whisp
Add 2 to the tens digit to get the ones digit for my flower.

Sunshine
My flower is a prime number between 38 and 55.

Cascadia
In my flower, if you subtract the tens digit from the ones digit, you get a difference of 1.

Ripple
If you multiply the digits in my flower, you get 24.

Ivy
My flower is even. It is greater than 55 and less than 60. It is <u>not</u> a multiple of 7.

37

58

42

38

59

53

46

56

49

Name _____

Dragons

What if dragons were real? Write 3 things that people might do.

1. _____

2. _____

3. _____

Use the clues to find the name of each dragon. Write each name near its description.

- **Flame** is smaller than **Talon**.

- **Scalia** lost all of her teeth when she tried to eat cement.

- **Talon** is bigger than **Scalia**.

_____ has spots.

_____ is the biggest.

_____ has the sharpest teeth.

It takes 57 weeks for dragons to hatch from their eggs. How many days is that?

_____ days

Adult dragons have 226 teeth. How many teeth do 9 dragons have?

_____ teeth

Your job is to take some of the dragon's treasure. You do <u>not</u> have any weapons. The dragon <u>never</u> leaves her cave without a reason. What is your plan?

_____

_____

_____

_____

_____

Dragons

How are an alligator and a dragon the same? How are they different?
Write 3 ways for each.

Same	Different

Describe what you think a dragon smells like. Use your imagination and be descriptive!

_____

_____

ANALOGIES

scales : dragon :: feathers : _____

dragon : fly :: fish : _____

cave : dragon :: hive : _____

Doug the Dragon is fond of knights. He ate 18 of them in 3 days! He ate half as many on the first day as he did on the second day. On the third day, he gorged himself by eating the same number of knights that he'd eaten in the first 2 days. How many knights did Doug eat on each day?

Day 1: _____   Day 2: _____   Day 3: _____

  Critical and Creative Thinking Activities • EMC 3394 • © Evan-Moor Corp.

Name _____

Dragons

You found a rather large egg in your backyard. A few weeks later, the egg hatched. You are now the owner of a baby dragon. Of course, you decide to keep it. Answer the questions about how you will manage to raise your new pet.

What will you name your dragon? _____

What will you feed it? _____

What are 3 challenges that you will have to face while raising your dragon?

1. _____

2. _____

3. _____

Draw your dragon.

What will you train your dragon to do?

_____

_____

_____

_____

What will you do with your dragon when it is full-grown?

_____

_____

_____

_____

Kings and Queens

You are the king or the queen of a fairy-tale kingdom. What are 3 things that you must do to keep your kingdom running smoothly?

1. _____

2. _____

3. _____

ANALOGIES

queen : woman :: prince : _____

king : rich :: peasant : _____

castle : king :: hut : _____

In most countries today, there are no kings. Instead, the people vote for their leaders. Do you think this is a better system than having a king or a queen?

_____ Why or why not? _____

_____

King Horace and Queen Anabella have 3 daughters. Each daughter has 8 gowns. Queen Anabella has twice as many gowns as her daughters do altogether. How many gowns do all 4 women have altogether?

_____ gowns

The oldest son gets to be king. George is older than Harry. George is younger than Edward. Edward is older than John. John is older than George. Who gets to be king?

_____

Who is next in line to the throne?

_____

Kings and Queens

You are the king or the queen. Your son, the prince, is charming, and many princesses wish to marry him. The laws of the kingdom do not allow the prince to choose his own bride. Design a contest for the princesses to compete in to win the prince's hand in marriage.

_____

_____

_____

_____

King Gregory the Greedy taxed his subjects two-thirds of everything they harvested from their small farms. Fill in the chart to show how much his tax collectors took from each of the peasants.

Peasant	Crop	Number of Baskets Harvested	Number of Baskets Taxed
Benjamin	barley	51	
Sarah	apples	84	
Thomas	corn	108	
Rebecca	potatoes	147	

King Gregory the Greedy has decided that he must have a new throne. The new throne will be studded with 147 rubies, 649 sapphires, 353 emeralds, and 111 diamonds. How many gems will be on the new throne?

_____ gems

Draw King Gregory the Greedy.

Kings and Queens

Each king and queen listed below rules a different kingdom. Read the clues and use the chart to find out which kingdom each of them rules. Make an **X** in a square when it <u>cannot</u> be an answer. Draw a circle when it is a correct answer.

	Kingdoms					
	Whynota	Pizzaland	Educatia	Duckland	Adventuria	Readaland
King Elliot						
Queen Risa						
King Donald						
Queen Andrea						
King Patrick						
Queen Wendy						

1. None of the kings or queens rules a land that begins with the same letter as his or her name.

2. The person who rules Educatia often visits her brother, who rules Duckland.

3. None of the women rules Pizzaland.

4. Last spring, King Patrick, Queen Andrea, and King Donald traveled to Readaland to attend the annual Festival of Books.

5. King Donald often goes to Adventuria and Pizzaland to visit friends.

Magic

Many authors have created mythical places where magic is possible. Some examples include Narnia, Oz, and Hogwarts. If you could visit a magical world, which one would you choose?

_____ Why? _____

_____

_____

Number the magical abilities from 1 to 8 according to how much you would like to have them. The one you would like the most should be number 1.

_____ fly

_____ turn people into stone

_____ move people and things

_____ turn invisible

_____ speak to animals

_____ predict the future

_____ make food appear

_____ turn straw into gold

Ana must give the evil witch 140 gold coins or the witch will turn Ana's husband into a frog. Luckily, Ana has a magic pot that makes 1 gold coin every 2 minutes. How long will it take to make all of the gold coins Ana needs?

_____ hours _____ minutes

Ana turned on the magic pot at 2:15. At what time will she have enough coins?

_____

Write a sentence using the words *magic*, *wizard*, *want*, and *spaghetti*.

_____

_____

Magic

If your best friend suddenly revealed that he or she could do magic, how would you feel?

_____

How would it change your friendship?

_____

_____

Use the clues to find the words that have to do with magic.

magic stick	w_____
witch's friend	c_____
magical liquid	p_____
Merlin is one	w_____
magic words	s_____
could be a prince	f_____

Use the clues to find the characters who can do magic.

Oz's good witch	G_____
Peter Pan's friend	T_____
Potter's pal	R_____
singing nanny	M_____
helped Cinderella	F_____
lives in a lamp	G_____

Alaina is 9 years old and has discovered that she can do magic. No one Alaina knows, including her parents and her sister, can do magic. What are 3 problems that the family might have to deal with?

1. _____

2. _____

3. _____

 Critical and Creative Thinking Activities • EMC 3394 • © Evan-Moor Corp.

Magic

Fill in the chart to tell what you would do with each magical item. Each item will work only one time.

Magical Item	What It Does	What You Will Use It For
key	will open any lock	
carpet	will take you anywhere in the world	
box	can be opened only by you	
book	will tell you anything you need to know	
pot	will make any food you want	
crystal ball	will allow you to see into the future	
cloak	will make you invisible	
potion I	will make someone tell the truth	
potion II	will make you super smart for one hour	
potion III	will turn you into any animal for one hour	

Name _____

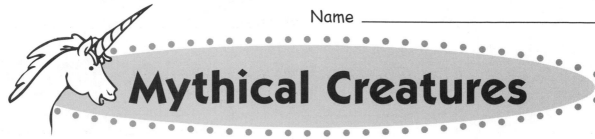

Mythical Creatures

Fill in the missing vowels for the mythical creatures. Then find the words in the word search. If you don't know the creature, try finding it in the word search first.

TR __ LL

C __ NT __ __ R

D R __ G __ N

F __ __ R Y

B __ S __ L __ S K

M __ R M __ __ D

__ L F

P H __ __ N __ X

G N __ M __

C Y C L __ P S

W __ R __ W __ L F

G __ B L __ N

__ N __ C __ R N

```
B  A  S  I  L  I  S  K  Y  K  B  G
P  B  A  F  L  O  W  E  R  E  W  O
V  C  I  M  O  L  V  M  U  D  G  B
Q  Y  X  N  R  P  Y  E  F  N  P  L
E  C  E  N  T  A  U  R  O  O  U  I
F  L  S  H  E  E  P  M  G  N  P  N
A  O  F  T  D  A  E  A  Y  I  P  H
I  P  P  H  O  E  N  I  X  S  Y  C
R  S  N  O  G  A  R  D  G  E  M  E
Y  L  I  O  N  N  R  O  C  I  N  U
```

Word Search Challenge:
Find 3 animals that are not mythical.

_____ _____ _____

Finish the tongue twisters.

Two terrible trolls _____

Gorf the Goofy Goblin _____

Meera Mermaid made _____

Willy Werewolf was _____

   Critical and Creative Thinking Activities • EMC 3394 • © Evan-Moor Corp.

Mythical Creatures

Norman Johnson turns into a werewolf on the full moon. There is a full moon once every 28 days. Today is April 23. It is a full moon. On what date will Norman turn into a werewolf again?

_____

Starla the Mermaid was collecting pearls to make a necklace. She collected 3 pearls each day for 4 weeks. How many pearls does Starla have?

_____ pearls

Add adjectives and adverbs to make each sentence more interesting.

The troll attacked the elf.

_____

The fairy landed on the flower.

_____

Some mythical creatures are two creatures combined. For example, a centaur is half man, half horse. Invent a mythical creature that is a combination of two real animals. Which two animals will you use?

_____

_____

What is this creature called?

_____

Draw your mythical creature.

Name _____

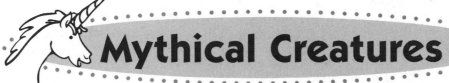
Mythical Creatures

What might happen if a mythical creature listed at the top of the chart were to suddenly meet up with a mythical creature listed on the side of the chart? Fill in the chart with one or two sentences in each square. Use your imagination!

	Troll	Unicorn
Fairy		
Dragon		
Centaur		

Choose one scenario from the chart and illustrate it.

Critical and Creative Thinking Activities • EMC 3394 • © Evan-Moor Corp.

My Bike

The seat is one part of a bicycle. How many other parts can you name?

1. _____   5. _____

2. _____   6. _____

3. _____   7. _____

4. _____   8. _____

Trace a path showing how you can visit 12 friends on your way home. You may <u>not</u> visit any house more than once or retrace your own path.

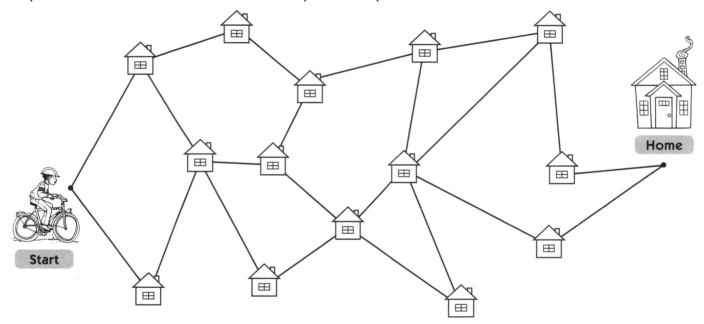

Complete each sentence.

My bike _____.

_____ my bike _____.

_____ my bike.

My Bike

Write a sentence about riding your bike. Include 1 adverb and 2 adjectives.

_____

You have 57 wheels. How many bicycles can you make?

_____ bicycles

How many tricycles can you make?

_____ tricycles

David rides his bike to school and home every day. His school is 3 miles away from his house. How many miles will he ride in 5 days?

_____ miles

In 8 days? _____ miles

What are 3 reasons you might choose <u>not</u> to ride your bike somewhere?

1. _____

2. _____

3. _____

Ally, Billy, Elaine, Richard, Nell, and John all have different color bikes. Read the clues and write each person's name next to the color of his or her bike.

- None of the girls has a white bike.

- Nell does <u>not</u> have a green bike.

- Two of the children have names that begin with the same letter as the color of their bikes.

- One of the girl's names ends in the letter that the color of her bike begins with.

blue _____

green _____

yellow _____

purple _____

red _____

white _____

Critical and Creative Thinking Activities • EMC 3394 • © Evan-Moor Corp.

Name _____

My Bike

Kevin wants a new bike. Solve the problems to see how he earns it.

1. The bike Kevin wants costs $170. He already has $25 left over from his birthday. How much more money will he need to earn? $_____

2. Kevin starts earning money by mowing lawns. He mows 3 lawns for his neighbors and gets $12 for each lawn. How much more money does he need to earn? $_____

3. The next day, Kevin picks blackberries for Mrs. Katz. She pays $1.50 for every tub of berries, plus a piece of blackberry pie! Kevin picks 8 tubs. How much more money does he need? $_____

4. Kevin spends all day Saturday cleaning out the garage. He is exhausted that night but managed to earn $35. How much more money does he need to earn? $_____

5. The next day, Kevin is too tired to do a job, but he does find $3 in change under the couch cushions. How much money does he need to earn now? $_____

6. Next, Kevin helps Mr. Casey haul wood chips for his garden. Mr. Casey pays $4 for every wheelbarrow full of wood chips. Kevin hauls 7 loads of chips. How much more money does he need? $_____

7. Next, Kevin baby-sits the Tanner twins. They nearly drive him crazy, but he makes $18 plus a $5 tip. How much money does he need to earn now? $_____

8. Kevin decides to earn the last few dollars by selling lemonade. He plans to sell each cup for a quarter. How many cups will he need to sell in order to earn the rest of the money? _____

9. Kevin finally has all the money he needs! His parents are proud of his hard work and buy him a new helmet for $24, a bike lock for $18, and a water bottle for $8. Including the new bike, how much money does Kevin's family spend at the bike store? $_____

My Pencil

Write 6 adjectives to describe your pencil.

1. _____   4. _____

2. _____   5. _____

3. _____   6. _____

What is the name of the company that made your pencil? _____

Tori and Luke have a lot of new pencils. They have decided to see how long their classroom is in pencils. Each pencil is exactly 8 inches long. It takes 45 pencils to reach from one side of the room to the other. How many feet long is the classroom?

_____ feet

Every time Perry sharpens his pencil, it gets half an inch shorter. His pencil was 8 inches long when it was new. How many times can he sharpen it before it gets shorter than 2 inches?

_____ times

Perry throws away his pencil when it is 2 inches long. If Perry sharpens his pencil one time every 3 days, how long will it last?

_____ days

Continue the pattern (look carefully, it is tricky).

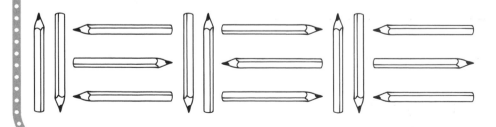

Name _____

My Pencil

Which do you like better—traditional wooden pencils or mechanical pencils?

_____ Why? _____

_____

What materials were used to make your pencil?

_____

_____

_____

_____

_____

Try to balance your pencil on your finger for 10 seconds.

Could you do it?

☐ yes

☐ no

Draw a realistic picture of your pencil.

Besides writing and erasing, what are some other things that you can do with a pencil?

1. _____

2. _____

3. _____

4. _____

5. _____

6. _____

How many pencils are in your desk right now?

Guess: _____   Actual number: _____

My Pencil

What would these everyday objects say if they could talk?

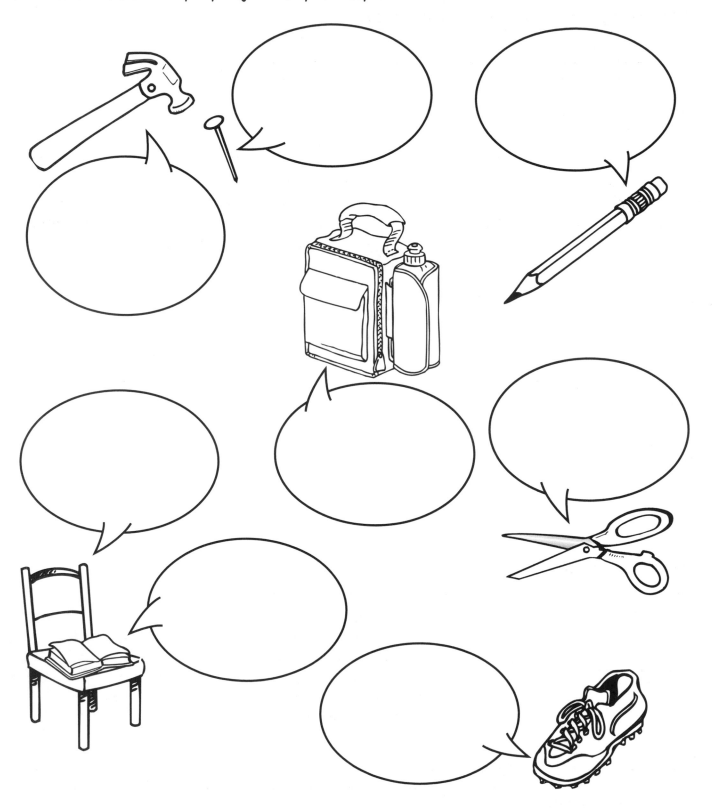

Name _____

My Hands

Write 4 adjectives to describe your hands.

1. _____   3. _____

2. _____   4. _____

How many fingers
(not including thumbs) are in
your classroom right now?

_____ fingers

Grandma has decided to knit mittens for all of
her grandchildren. She has 9 grandchildren.
It takes 3 hours to make one mitten. How many
hours of knitting will it take Grandma to make
all of the mittens?

_____ hours

What are 3 things that would be much harder to do if you did <u>not</u> have thumbs?

1. _____

2. _____

3. _____

What do they say?

HAhand**ND**

_____

hand hand hand
hand hand hand
‾‾‾‾‾‾‾‾‾‾‾‾‾‾‾
DECK

_____

H H H
A A A
N N N
D D D
M M M
E E E

_____

Name _____

 # My Hands

What does each expression mean?

"It's out of my hands." _____

"I did it with my bare hands." _____

"She has the upper hand." _____

"A bird in the hand is worth two in the bush." _____

_____

ANALOGIES

hand : wrist :: foot : _____

fingers : ten :: ears : _____

glove : hand :: sock : _____

boy : hand :: kitten : _____

Why do you think we have fingernails?

_____

Why do you think most people can't bend their fingers backward?

_____

Do you think it is okay to tell a lie if you cross your fingers behind your back? _____

    Why or why not? _____

What is the sound of one hand clapping? _____

     Critical and Creative Thinking Activities • EMC 3394 • © Evan-Moor Corp.

Name _____

 # My Hands

What kinds of fingerprints do you have? Follow the instructions to find out!

- Use a pencil to fill in the square on the right. Press hard and make it dark. You may need to go over it again as you make more prints.

- Press one of your fingertips on the square.

- Stick a piece of clear tape onto your fingertip.

- Place the tape in the box for that finger to see your print!

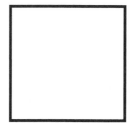

	Thumb	Index	Middle	Ring	Pinkie
RIGHT HAND					

	Thumb	Index	Middle	Ring	Pinkie
LEFT HAND					

Look at the different kinds of fingerprints below to help you identify yours. Label each of your prints with the appropriate number.

   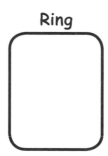 

1	2	3	4	5	6	7
Loop	Double Loop	Central Pocket Loop	Plain Arch	Tented Arch	Plain Whorl	Accidental

Which kind of fingerprint do you have the most of? _____

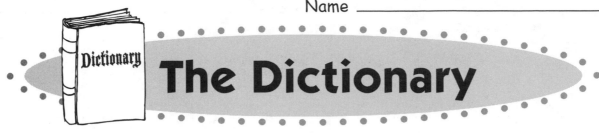

The Dictionary

What are 3 things that you can use a dictionary for?

1. _____

2. _____

3. _____

Write a definition that you might find in a dictionary for the word *dictionary*.

_____

_____

Richard has decided to read the entire dictionary. His plan is to read one page each day. There are 1,825 pages in Richard's dictionary. Make an **X** on the number line to show about how many years it will take Richard to read the entire book.

```
+----+----+----+----+----+----+----+----+
0    1    2    3    4    5    6    7    8
```

Ian has a different plan. He has decided to read 3 words in the dictionary each day. If both boys start on the same day, how many words will Ian have read when Richard is done?

_____ words

If your name were in the dictionary, what word would be directly above it? What word would be directly below it?

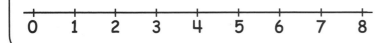 and _____

A large dictionary has about 500,000 words and definitions.
How many do you think you know? _____

How many do you think your teacher knows? _____

 Critical and Creative Thinking Activities • EMC 3394 • © Evan-Moor Corp.

The Dictionary

Make as many smaller words as you can from the letters in this word:

DICTIONARY

1. _____   6. _____   11. _____

2. _____   7. _____   12. _____

3. _____   8. _____   13. _____

4. _____   9. _____   14. _____

5. _____   10. _____   15. _____

Would you rather use a dictionary in book form or a dictionary on the Internet?

_____ Why? _____

_____

You do not know how to spell a word and need to look it up in the dictionary. Number the steps that you must take from 1 to 6.

_____ Scan the page for your word.

_____ Get the dictionary.

_____ Find your word.

_____ Write down the word correctly.

_____ Use the guide words to find the correct page.

_____ Open the dictionary to the letter your word begins with.

Jessica made a stack of dictionaries in her classroom. She used 28 dictionaries. The stack was 7 feet high. How many inches thick was each dictionary?

_____ inches

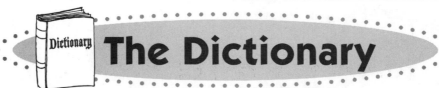

The Dictionary

In a dictionary, the guide words at the top of a page are the same as the first and last words on that page. For each pair of guide words below, write 3 other words that would appear on that page of the dictionary.

Guide Words	3 Words That Would Appear on the Page		
car, comb	_____	_____	_____
vanilla, voice	_____	_____	_____
mindless, more	_____	_____	_____
tape, tiger	_____	_____	_____
nobody, nothing	_____	_____	_____
wild, write	_____	_____	_____
brand, bright	_____	_____	_____
arid, attract	_____	_____	_____

Locks and Keys

What are 10 things that you might need to open with a key?

1. _____
2. _____
3. _____
4. _____
5. _____

6. _____
7. _____
8. _____
9. _____
10. _____

Use the clues to find the words. Each word rhymes with either *LOCK* or *KEY*.

has a trunk _____

stone _____

to speak _____

look _____

on your leg _____

on your foot _____

hot drink _____

tells the time _____

group of sheep _____

not a prisoner _____

Shelby has a combination lock for her bike. Use the clues to find her combination.

- The combination is a 3-digit number.

- The first and third digits are even.

- The middle digit is 3 more than the last digit.

- The middle digit is 7 more than the first digit.

- If you add all of the digits together, you get 17.

What is Shelby's combination?

_____

Name _____

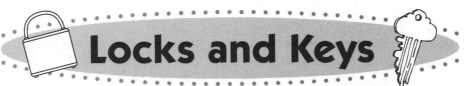
Locks and Keys

Do you think it is a good idea to have a secret house key hidden somewhere near your house?

_____ Why or why not? _____

_____

Why do you think keys are usually made from metal instead of plastic or wood?

_____

_____

What do these say?

key
key key
key key key key
key key key key
key key key key

_____

K
C O   U go
L

_____

KEY

_____

What are 3 reasons a person might decide <u>not</u> to lock the door when he or she leaves the house?

1. _____

2. _____

3. _____

Write a sentence using the words *lock*, *key*, *secret*, and *watermelon*.

_____

  Critical and Creative Thinking Activities • EMC 3394 • © Evan-Moor Corp.

Name _____

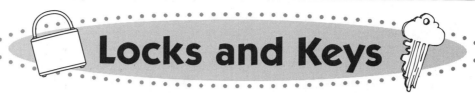

Locks and Keys

Each key opens a lock. Each key and lock pair will form a 4-letter word. Match the keys and locks, and then write the words on the lines. Use each key and each lock <u>only</u> one time.

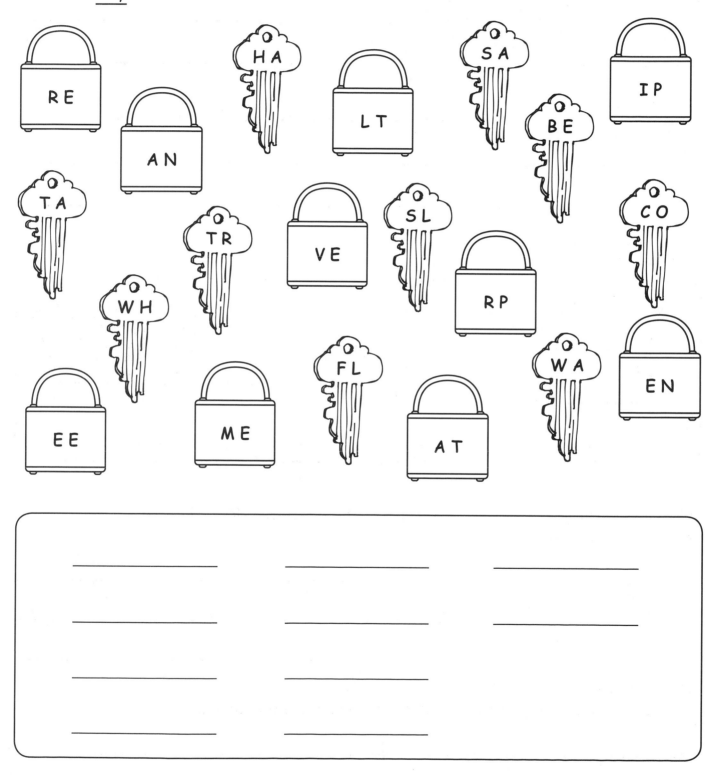

Thank you.

Manners

You're welcome.

Do you think that manners are important? _____

Why or why not? _____

_____

Do you think that it is possible to be too polite? _____

Why or why not? _____

_____

Find the word for each clue. Each word is made from the letters in this word:

PLEASE

friend _____

ocean _____

long, skinny fish _____

liquid in a tree _____

aquatic mammal _____

do this to an orange _____

half price _____

do at night _____

light-colored _____

Aunt Clara is more polite than Aunt Edna. Aunt Edna is less polite than Aunt Martha. Aunt Petunia is just plain rude.

Write **T** if the statement is **true**, **F** if it is **false**, and **C** if you **can't tell**.

_____ Aunt Martha is more polite than Aunt Edna.

_____ Aunt Clara is the most polite aunt.

_____ Aunt Martha might be more polite than Aunt Clara.

_____ Aunt Petunia is less polite than Aunt Edna.

_____ Aunt Petunia never says "please."

Manners

Thank you.

You're welcome.

Do you have better table manners at home or at a friend's house? _____

Why? _____

_____

Carrie is having dinner with a new friend and her family. She does <u>not</u> like the food. What should Carrie do?

_____

Number the table manners from 1 to 7. The one you think is most important should be number 1.

_____ saying "please" and "thank you"

_____ not slurping soup

_____ not reaching for things

_____ chewing with your mouth closed

_____ keeping elbows off the table

_____ using silverware correctly

_____ using a quiet voice

Would you rather have a friend who always interrupted you when you were talking or one who always chewed with his or her mouth open?

_____

Why? _____

_____

_____

_____

Brent usually has excellent table manners, but tonight, his manners are terrible. List 3 possible reasons.

1. _____

2. _____

3. _____

Manners

Thank you.   *You're welcome.*

Dana decided to do an experiment. Each day for a week, she kept track of all the times she said "please," "thank you," and "you're welcome." Use the chart to answer the questions.

	Mon.	Tues.	Wed.	Thurs.	Fri.	Sat.	Sun.
Please	2	5	6	8	9	14	12
Thank you	2	3	6	2	7	10	11
You're welcome	1	1	3	5	7	7	4

On which day did Dana say "please" the most? _____

When you consider the whole week, did Dana say "please," "thank you," or "you're welcome" the most?

_____ How many times? _____

How many times during the week did Dana say "you're welcome"? _____

What is the average number of times per day Dana said "you're welcome"? _____

What do you notice about how Dana's behavior changed throughout the week?

_____

Why do you think this happened?

_____

Use the grid to make a bar graph showing how many times Dana said each phrase on Saturday.

```
         0   2   4   6   8   10  12  14  16  18  20  22  24  26
```

Critical and Creative Thinking Activities • EMC 3394 • © Evan-Moor Corp.

Hats and Caps

What is the main difference between a hat and a cap?

_____

_____

What are 5 different reasons a person might wear a hat?

1. _____

2. _____

3. _____

4. _____

5. _____

Jeremy wears his baseball cap every Friday. Taylor wears his baseball cap every other day. Today is Friday, April 3. Both boys are wearing their caps. How many days will it be until both boys are wearing their caps on the same day again?

_____ days

What date will it be? _____

Mike the Magician can pull rabbits out of his hat. Yesterday, he pulled out three times as many rabbits as he did today. He pulled 68 rabbits out of his hat altogether. How many did he pull out on each day?

Yesterday: _____

Today: _____

Skyler wants to ride his bike, but he cannot find his bike helmet. What should he do?

_____

_____

Name _____

Hats and Caps

What are 4 different reasons a person might wear a helmet?

1. _____

2. _____

3. _____

4. _____

Use the clues to find the words. Each word rhymes with either *HAT* or *CAP*.

furry pet _____

to sleep in the day _____

to touch lightly _____

conversation _____

noise with hands _____

for baseball _____

spoiled child _____

navigation tool _____

open-handed hit _____

Cody wears a different color baseball cap to school each day. The colors are green, yellow, blue, orange, and red. He wears primary colors on the first 3 days of the week. He does <u>not</u> wear a green cap on Friday. He does <u>not</u> wear a red cap on Monday or Tuesday. He does <u>not</u> wear a yellow cap on Tuesday. Write the colors of the caps.

Monday: _____

Tuesday: _____

Wednesday: _____

Thursday: _____

Friday: _____

ANALOGIES

hard hat : construction worker :: stocking hat : _____

firefighter's helmet : red :: chef's hat : _____

head : hat :: waist : _____

        Critical and Creative Thinking Activities • EMC 3394 • © Evan-Moor Corp.

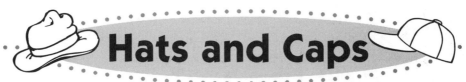

Hats and Caps

Whose hat is whose? Use the clues to find out. Make an **X** in a square when it <u>cannot</u> be an answer. Draw a circle when it is a correct answer.

		People					
		Marlon	Ginger	Fred	Marilyn	Clark	Judy
Hats	Firefighter's helmet						
	Graduation cap						
	Chef's hat						
	Winter stocking cap						
	Hard hat						
	Bike helmet						

1. Clark and Judy do <u>not</u> wear their hats when they work.

2. Marlon's hat has saved his life several times. Marlon lives in Hawaii.

3. The man who owns the stocking cap received it as a gift from his grandmother, who knit it just for him.

4. The women are all terrible cooks.

5. Judy is only 10 years old.

6. The person who owns the firefighter's helmet always keeps it close to her boots.

7. Ginger's hat matches her gown.

Name _____

Presents

Pretend that you can give any present you want to each of the people below. What will you give?

your best friend _____

your mom _____

your teacher _____

a blind child _____

a child in the hospital _____

the president _____

Laura got 16 presents for her birthday. Half of them were games. Three-fourths of the games were board games. How many board games did Laura get?

_____ board games

6 children got presents. Read the clues, and then write each child's name next to his or her present.

- Ethan's present does <u>not</u> have a bow.

- Josie's present is <u>not</u> the smallest.

- Mandy's present has dots. So does Aiden's.

- Kathy's and Josie's presents both have bows.

- Carlos's and Mandy's presents are both in gift bags.

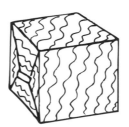

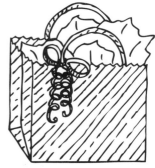

Name _____

Presents

What is the best present that you ever got? _____

Why? _____

_____

What is the best present that you ever gave? _____

Why? _____

_____

You receive a present in a long, skinny box. What are 4 things that might be inside?

1. _____

2. _____

3. _____

4. _____

Janie made her mom a present. It took her $4\frac{1}{2}$ hours to make it. She made the card, too. That took 45 minutes. It took 8 minutes to wrap the gift. Janie started her project at 10:15 in the morning. At what time did she finish?

_____

"Good things come in small packages."

What do you think this expression means?

_____

What are 3 good things that could come in small packages?

1. _____   2. _____   3. _____

Name _____

Presents

Fill in the crossword puzzle with things that you might receive as gifts.

DOWN

1 Take a picture
2 A favorite stuffed toy
3 Use to tell the time
4 Play it with a friend
8 Wear when chilly
9 Bounce and balance
11 Spins around and around your middle
12 One for each hand
13 Keeps your pants up
15 Many pieces
16 Watch while eating popcorn

ACROSS

5 Need a bat
6 Use on a windy day
7 Hang on the wall
10 See at night
14 Need a helmet
15 Wear at night
17 Read me
18 Bright colors
19 Meows

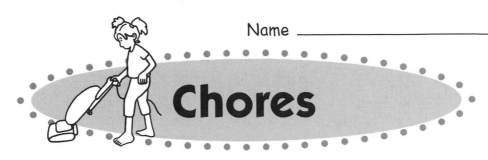

Chores

Do you think that children should have chores to do each day? _____

Why or why not? _____

_____

Should children be paid for doing chores? _____

Why or why not? _____

_____

The list of chores below has gotten all mixed up! Rewrite it so that each verb goes with the correct noun.

Chores

dust the dog _____

dry the garden _____

fold the windows _____

get the counters _____

weed the floor _____

feed the laundry _____

wash the mail _____

make the furniture _____

wipe the bed _____

sweep the dishes _____

Mark lives on a farm. Every morning, he spends 28 minutes milking the cow. Then he spends 17 minutes feeding the chickens and collecting the eggs. It takes him 54 minutes to feed the horses and shovel out the stalls. How long does it take Mark to do his chores?

_____ minutes

If Mark starts at 6:30 in the morning, at what time will he be done?

_____

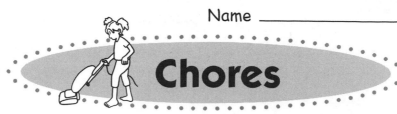

Chores

What is a good chore for...

a 3-year-old? _____

a 5-year-old? _____

an 8-year-old? _____

a 10-year-old? _____

a 13-year-old? _____

John, Jake, and Jim must weed the garden. There are 15 rows to weed. It takes half an hour to weed 1 row. How long will it take the three boys to weed the whole garden?

_____ hours

ANALOGIES

towel : dishes :: mop : _____

sweep : broom :: weed : _____

chore : home :: test : _____

Christine is very good about doing her chores every day. Yesterday, she did not do any of her chores. List 3 possible reasons.

1. _____

2. _____

3. _____

"Many hands make light work."

What do you think this expression means? _____

_____

Name _____

Chores

The Johnsons use a chore chart to show which chores each of their 4 children will do each week. Read the rules, and then fill in the chart with the children's names.

| Kelsey | Tom | Amelia | Maya |

	Monday	Tuesday	Wednesday	Thursday	Friday
Empty the dishwasher					
Set the table					
Help with dinner					
Fold laundry					
Feed the cats					
Sweep the floors					
Take out the garbage					
Tidy the living room					

1. Kelsey is 11 and Tom is 9, so they each do three chores a day. Amelia and Maya are 5-year-old twins, so they each do just one chore a day.

2. Amelia and Maya each do a different chore each day, but they do <u>not</u> take out the garbage, sweep the floors, or tidy the living room.

3. Both Kelsey and Tom must do each chore at least one time a week.

4. No child may do the same chore two days in a row.

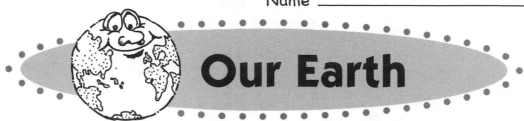

Our Earth

Where is your favorite place on Earth? _____

If the Earth could talk, what do you think it would say?

Number the places from 1 to 8 according to how much you would like to visit them. The one you would like to visit the most should be number 1.

_____ China

_____ Africa

_____ Australia

_____ France

_____ Peru

_____ Egypt

_____ India

_____ Hawaii

A natural resource is something we use that comes from nature. Coal is an example of a natural resource. How many other natural resources can you name?

1. _____

2. _____

3. _____

4. _____

5. _____

6. _____

7. _____

8. _____

9. _____

Name _____

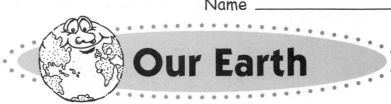

Our Earth

How does recycling help the Earth?

_____

How does driving less help the Earth?

_____

How does using less electricity help the Earth?

_____

If you could fly around the Earth in an airplane, you would have to fly 24,900 miles. An airplane flies about 500 miles an hour. About how many hours would it take you to circle the Earth?

_____ hours

Where in the world are you?

Continent: _____

Country: _____

State: _____

County: _____

City: _____

Street: _____

Add 2 more each time, and then tell what they are.

Atlantic, Indian, _____, _____ What? _____

Australia, Asia, _____, _____ What? _____

Sahara, Death Valley, _____, _____ What? _____

France, Spain, Belgium, _____, _____ What? _____

Cuba, Hawaii, New Zealand, _____, _____ What? _____

Our Earth

Use the initials and the clues to help you name the landmarks and places.

in New York   S_____ of L_____

in Paris   E_____ T_____

in Egypt   G_____ P_____

piranhas live here   A_____ R_____

tallest mountain   M_____ E_____

smallest continent   A_____

very big hole   G_____ C_____

where movie stars live   H_____

cold continent   A_____

European country that is shaped like a boot   I_____

home of Old Faithful   Y_____

where Mickey Mouse lives   D_____

United States' neighbor to the north   C_____

where the president of the USA lives   the W_____ H_____

largest of the Great Lakes   L_____ S_____

largest state in the U.S.   A_____

big, beautiful white building in India   T_____ M_____

volcano in northwest USA   M_____ S_____ H_____

big barrier in Asia   G_____ W_____ of C_____

big body of water   P_____ O_____

Garbage

Write a sentence that is always true about garbage.

_____

Write a sentence that is sometimes true about garbage.

_____

Write a sentence that is never true about garbage.

_____

Find the word for each clue. Each word is made from the letters in this word:

GARBAGE

use to carry things _____

to snatch _____

large, furry animal _____

how old you are _____

to boast _____

flat boat _____

Each person in the United States produces about 1,609 pounds of garbage a year! About how many pounds of garbage did your family produce last year?

_____ pounds

About how many pounds of garbage have you produced in your life so far?

_____ pounds

What are 3 ways that your family could produce less garbage?

1. _____

2. _____

3. _____

Garbage

When we reuse things instead of throwing them away, we save resources and we don't fill up landfills. How could you reuse each of these items?

soda bottle _____

egg carton _____

old magazines _____

torn shirt _____

old CDs and DVDs _____

SYNONYMS

Garbage is a synonym for *trash*. Write a synonym for each word below.

bin _____

smelly _____

slimy _____

broken _____

soiled _____

disgusting _____

Mr. Smith takes out his garbage on Mondays and Thursdays.
Mr. Jones takes out his garbage once every 3 days. Both men have taken out their garbage today. Today is Thursday, March 6. On what date will both men take out their garbage on the same day again?

_____

What are 3 bad things that would happen if no one ever took out the garbage?

1. _____

2. _____

3. _____

 Critical and Creative Thinking Activities • EMC 3394 • © Evan-Moor Corp.

 Garbage

Some archaeologists study the garbage of ancient cultures to learn about how people lived. What can you learn about the Smith family by studying their garbage? Write about it below.

Found in Smith Family's Garbage and Recycling

- rice cakes bag
- diet soda bottle
- wilted lettuce leaves
- carrot peelings
- tomato stems
- broken mousetrap
- chocolate cake mix box
- frosting container
- 10 half-burned candles
- crumpled wrapping paper
- ice-cream carton
- school lunch calendar
- town pool schedule
- sugarless gum wrappers
- dead flowers
- *American Girl* magazine
- *Boys' Life* magazine
- 3 dog food cans
- large pizza box
- lice shampoo bottle
- tofu container
- nonfat yogurt container
- allergy pill bottle
- microwave popcorn bag
- broken Beatles CD
- veggie burger box
- hamburger bun bag
- onion skins
- 2 lottery tickets
- unidentifiable moldy stuff

What are 5 things that you know about this family?

1. _____

2. _____

3. _____

4. _____

5. _____

What are 5 things that are probably true about this family?

1. _____

2. _____

3. _____

4. _____

5. _____

What are 5 things that might be true about this family?

1. _____

2. _____

3. _____

4. _____

5. _____

Colorific!

The answer is **purple**. What is the question?

_____

The answer is **yellow and black**. What is the question?

_____

Unscramble the names of the colors, and then write them in the grid.

B
L
A
C
K

WORBN _____

GENER _____

TEWIH _____

PRECOP _____

GRONAE _____

DRE _____   RAGY _____   LEPRUP _____

LUBE _____   KINP _____   LIVERS _____

LOGD _____   CLKAB _____   WOLELY _____

Colorific!

Why do you think many fire engines and all stop signs are red?

_____

Why do you think people who work in a hospital often wear white?

_____

Anna has 3 shirts: yellow, orange, and red. She has 3 pairs of pants: blue, purple, and green. How many different combinations of shirts and pants can Anna make?

_____ combinations

If you put 6 blue marbles, 6 yellow marbles, and 6 red marbles in a bag, what are the chances of getting a blue marble the first time you choose one?

_____

How many times would you have to draw from the bag to be sure you chose a blue marble?

_____

What are 3 problems that you would have if you could see only in black and white?

1. _____

2. _____

3. _____

ANALOGIES

yellow : school bus :: green : _____

primary : blue :: secondary : _____

red : embarrassed :: green : _____

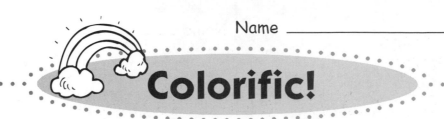

Colorific!

Here is a fun trick to play on your brain. Use **red**, **blue**, **yellow**, **green**, **orange**, **purple**, and **brown** to neatly color each of these color names. But do <u>not</u> color them with the correct colors. For example, do <u>not</u> color the word *red* with **red**. When you are done, try to say the colors of the words as fast as you can. Do not read the words, just say the colors. Can you do it?

RED YELLOW

PURPLE GREEN

ORANGE BLUE

BROWN PURPLE

ORANGE GREEN

Why do you think it is so hard to say the color names? _____

_____

Cats and Dogs

Fill in the Venn diagram with at least 3 things in each section.

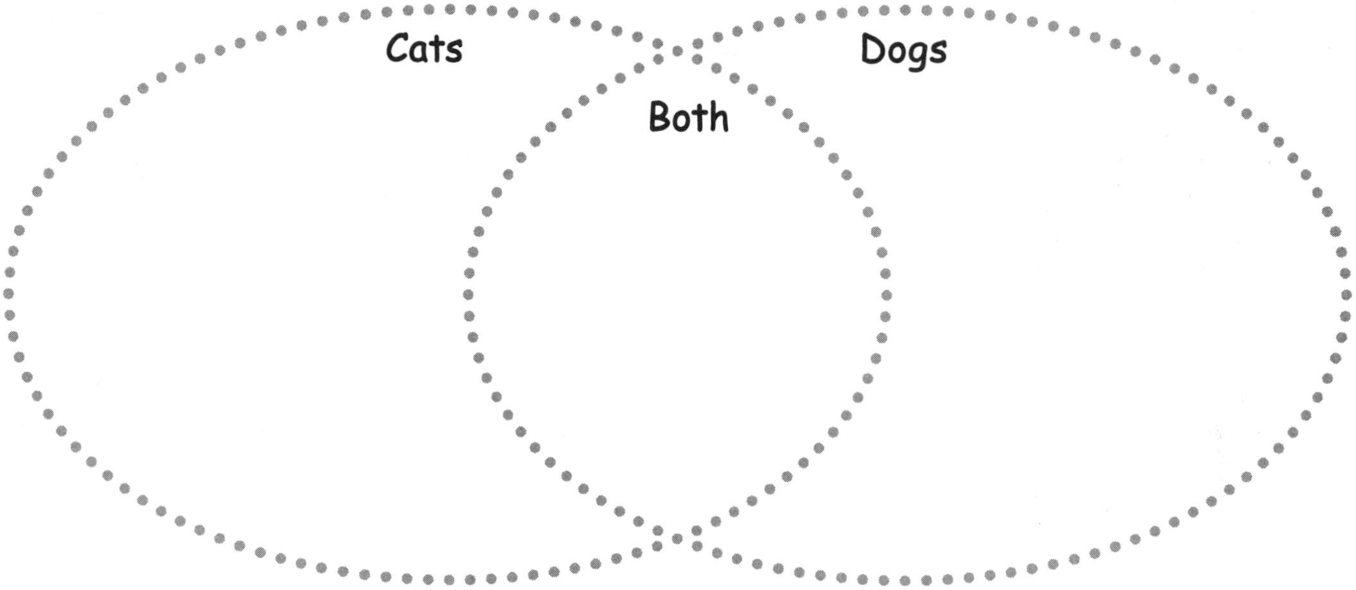

Cats   **Dogs**

Both

Would you rather have a cat or a dog for a pet? _____

List 3 reasons.

1. _____

2. _____

3. _____

Add adjectives and adverbs to make each sentence more interesting.

The dog barked at the girl.

_____

The kitten batted at the yarn.

_____

Cats and Dogs

What do you think these expressions mean?

"Curiosity killed the cat."

_____

"You can't teach an old dog new tricks."

_____

Fluffy the Cat had 6 kittens. Each of her kittens had 6 kittens. Each of those kittens had 6 kittens. How many cats are there altogether?

_____ cats

Marty's dog eats $\frac{2}{3}$ pound of dog food every day. Marty has bought a 25-pound bag of dog food. How many days will it last?

_____ days

Will there be any left over? _____

How many different dog breeds can you name?

1. _____ 5. _____ 9. _____

2. _____ 6. _____ 10. _____

3. _____ 7. _____ 11. _____

4. _____ 8. _____ 12. _____

Why do you think most dogs can be trained to come, sit, stay, and even do tricks, while most cats cannot be easily trained to do those things?

_____

_____

Cats and Dogs

Pretend that you get to adopt a kitten or a puppy. Answer the questions about how you will care for your new pet.

Will you get a kitten or a puppy? _____ Male or female? _____

What will you name him or her? _____

What supplies will you need to take care of your new pet?

_____   _____   _____

_____   _____   _____

What are 3 challenges that you may have with your new pet. How will you deal with these challenges?

1. Challenge: _____

Solution: _____

2. Challenge: _____

Solution: _____

3. Challenge: _____

Solution: _____

What are 2 things that you look forward to doing with your new pet?

1. _____

_____

2. _____

_____

Draw your new pet.

Lost and Found

You don't have a cellphone. What is the best thing to do if you get lost...

at the mall? _____

at an amusement park? _____

in the woods? _____

What is something that would be...

bad to lose? _____   bad to find? _____

easy to lose? _____   hard to find? _____

hard to lose? _____   cool to find? _____

Use the clues to find things that can be easy to lose. Then find them in the word search.

need for car and house   K_____

it can't buy happiness   M_____

wear when it is cold   C_____

for the TV   R_____   C_____

type of jewelry   E_____

furry friend   D_____ , C_____

chess or checkers   G_____

on a diet   W_____

to take a chance   B_____

need it for school   P_____

R	M	K	E	Y	S	W
E	O	H	V	S	E	K
M	K	B	A	I	Q	E
O	H	W	G	O	U	A
T	Z	H	C	E	C	R
E	T	G	S	A	O	R
C	O	A	T	A	K	I
O	T	M	F	L	A	N
N	M	E	E	I	B	G
T	Q	O	N	C	O	O
R	D	U	N	N	P	D
O	A	R	W	E	R	H
L	B	E	T	P	Y	J

          Critical and Creative Thinking Activities • EMC 3394 • © Evan-Moor Corp.

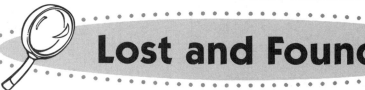

Lost and Found

Write a sentence about losing something. Use exactly 11 words.

_____

Write a sentence about finding something. Use exactly 7 words.

_____

Ethan found some shells at the beach. He lost one-third of them on his way back home. When he got home, he threw 4 of the shells away because they were broken. Then he gave half of the shells that were left to his mother. That left Ethan with 7 shells. How many shells did he originally find at the beach?

_____ shells

Joe lost his friend's phone number. He remembers that the first 3 digits are **555**. Use the clues to help Joe find the last 4 digits.

- All 4 digits are odd.

- The first and last digits are the same.

- The second and third digits add up to 14. So do the digits on each end.

- The second digit is the largest.

555 – ☐ ☐ ☐ ☐

"Finders keepers, losers weepers."

What does this expression mean? _____

_____

Do you agree? _____ Why or why not? _____

_____

Name _____

Lost and Found

Pretend that you are going on a scavenger hunt in your classroom. Answer each question below to see if you can find the item or the information.

1. What is something in your classroom with exactly 3 colors? _____

2. How many legs (people, tables, chairs, animals) are in your classroom? _____

3. What is something in your classroom that begins with **S**? _____

4. Who in your classroom can play the piano? _____

5. What is your teacher's middle name? _____

6. What letter is to the right of **E** on a keyboard? _____

7. What is the capitol of Peru? _____

8. How many inches tall is your desk? _____

9. What is something soft in your classroom? _____

10. On what day of the week is your birthday this year? _____

11. Which letter is the 19th in the alphabet? _____

12. What in your classroom are there more than 100 of? _____

13. What is the last word in the dictionary? _____

14. Who in your classroom will have the next birthday? _____

15. How many lights are in your classroom? _____

16. What is being served for hot lunch today? _____

17. What company published your math book? _____

18. How many minutes are there until your next recess? _____

Up, Up, and Away!

How many things can you think of that fly, float, or hover?

1. _____   5. _____   9. _____

2. _____   6. _____   10. _____

3. _____   7. _____   11. _____

4. _____   8. _____   12. _____

Draw and color a hot-air balloon for the basket.

• The balloon is blue.

• There is a yellow smiley face in the center.

• There is a circle of 12 orange dots around the face.

• There are 2 green horizontal stripes, one above the smiley face and one below it.

ANALOGIES

airplane : fly :: boat : _____

airplane : fuel :: kite : _____

sparrow : bird :: Superman : _____

bat : cave :: bee : _____

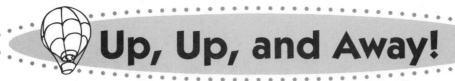 Up, Up, and Away!

How many 4-letter words can you make with the letters in this word:

HELICOPTER

1. _____   5. _____   9. _____

2. _____   6. _____   10. _____

3. _____   7. _____   11. _____

4. _____   8. _____   12. _____

Write something that is true about airplanes but <u>not</u> true about helicopters.

_____

Write something that is true about helicopters but <u>not</u> true about airplanes.

_____

Number the things that fly from 1 to 6 according to how much you would like to ride in them. The one you like the most should be number 1.

_____ airplane

_____ hot-air balloon

_____ space shuttle

_____ helicopter

_____ blimp

_____ hang glider

Mr. Olson is flying from Seattle to New York. His flight is supposed to depart Seattle at 8:42 and arrive in Chicago at 1:22. From Chicago, he will take a connecting flight at 2:19. Unfortunately, the first flight ran 43 minutes late. It will take Mr. Olson 16 minutes to get from the arrival gate to the departure gate in Chicago.

Will Mr. Olson make his connecting flight?

_____

By how many minutes will he miss it, or how many minutes will he have to spare?

_____ minutes

Name _____

Up, Up, and Away!

Six people are all flying to different cities. Use the clues to find out who is going where. Make an **X** in a square when it <u>cannot</u> be an answer. Draw a circle when it is a correct answer.

	People					
Cities	Carly	John	Joni	Paul	Diana	George
New York, USA						
Mexico City, Mexico						
London, England						
Paris, France						
Tokyo, Japan						
Sydney, Australia						

1. John lent his English-Japanese dictionary to the man who is going to Tokyo.

2. Joni and Paul are both going to Europe.

3. The woman who is going to Mexico City already knows Spanish.

4. The man who is going to England wanted to bring his daughter, whose name has 2 syllables, but she already has plans to visit friends in Australia.

Help!

Who in your family needs the most help? _____

Why? _____

SYNONYMS

Help is a synonym for *assist*. Write a synonym for each word below.

job _____

quick _____

ask _____

problem _____

shy _____

thankful _____

Last night, Terry helped his little sister with her homework. Use the clues to find out how long it took.

• It took less than an hour, but more than half an hour.

• The number of minutes is divisible by 5 but not by 10.

• The sum of the digits is 9.

Terry helped his sister for

_____ minutes.

Kate, Emily, and Lucy are working on a school project together. Kate is not doing her share of the work. In fact, she is not helping at all. What are 3 things that Emily and Lucy can do to solve this problem?

1. _____

2. _____

3. _____

Write a sentence using the words *help*, *ask*, *math*, and *tiger*.

_____

Help!

Jessica is having trouble with her math homework, but she won't ask anyone to help her. Give 3 possible reasons why she won't ask for help.

1. _____

2. _____

3. _____

Joanie helped her dad make cookies. They could fit 16 cookies on a cookie sheet (16 cookies = 1 batch). They had enough dough to make 200 cookies. How many batches did they make?

_____ batches

Jacob's mom helped him build a treehouse. For 3 weeks, they worked on the treehouse for 6 hours on Saturdays and for 2 hours after school on Mondays, Wednesdays, and Fridays. How many hours did Jacob work on the treehouse?

_____ hours

Benny is 6 years old. Every day, he makes a big mess in his room. Every evening, when it is time to clean up, he begs his mom to help him. Should Benny's mom help him?

_____ Why or why not? _____

_____

Name something that you once needed help with but do not need help with now.

_____

Name something that you need help with now but probably will not need help with when you are a little older.

_____

Name _____

Help!

Andrea's mom is planning a surprise birthday party for Andrea's dad. Andrea is helping by going to the store to buy what they will need. But Andrea's mom has written the shopping list in code (just in case it was found by the wrong person!). Help Andrea decode the list by replacing each letter with the one that comes 3 letters after it in the alphabet.

Example: **C** = **F** and **X** = **A**

Shopping List in Code	Decoded List
Z X K A I B P	_____
P Q O B X J B O P	_____
M X O Q V E X Q P	_____
Y X I I L L K P	_____
Z X H B	_____
F Z B Z O B X J	_____
M L Q X Q L Z E F M P	_____
M O B Q W B I P	_____
P L A X	_____
I B J L K X A B	_____
M X M B O M I X Q B P	_____
M I X P Q F Z C L O H P	_____
K X M H F K P	_____
Z L K C B Q Q F	_____

136   Critical and Creative Thinking Activities • EMC 3394 • © Evan-Moor Corp.

Name _____

Sticky Stuff

What are 8 things that tape is used for?

1. _____   5. _____

2. _____   6. _____

3. _____   7. _____

4. _____   8. _____

Use the clues to find sticky things.

in a stick or a bottle   G_____

on a sandwich   P_____

from the bees   H_____

comes on a roll   T_____

blow a bubble   G_____

goes on pancakes   S_____

from a tree   S_____

use to make cookies   D_____

You would not want to find honey on a computer keyboard. What are 7 other places where it would be very bad to find honey?

1. _____

2. _____

3. _____

4. _____

5. _____

6. _____

7. _____

Write a sentence using the words *gum*, *bubble*, *stuck*, and *shoe*.

_____

Write a sentence about molasses. Use exactly 8 words.

_____

Sticky Stuff

Which is better, glue in a bottle or glue in a stick? _____

Why? _____

Is it better to take off a bandage quickly or slowly? _____

Why? _____

In September, Penelope ate a peanut butter sandwich every Monday, Wednesday, and Friday. September started on a Wednesday. How many peanut butter sandwiches did she eat altogether?

_____ peanut butter sandwiches

In September, Penelope's brother Henry ate a honey sandwich every 4th day. How many sandwiches did he eat altogether?

_____ honey sandwiches

Emma keeps bees and sells the honey. She sells a jar of honey for $4.75. Yesterday, she sold twice as much honey as she did today. She made $133 dollars yesterday. How many jars of honey did Emma sell yesterday?

_____ jars of honey

How many jars did Emma sell today?

_____ jars of honey

How much money did Emma make today?

$_____

The answer is **try using some tape**. What is the question?

_____

The answer is **melted chocolate**. What is the question?

_____

Sticky Stuff

Sandy is the owner of Sandy's Candy, where she sells only yummy, sticky, sweet things. Use the price chart to answer the questions about what some of her customers bought.

Sandy's Candy

Caramel Corn	Small ... $2.50
	Large ... $3.75
Cotton Candy....................	$3.50
Marshmallow Squares	$2.25
Caramel Apple..................	$2.75
Saltwater Taffy ...... 12 pieces/$1.00	

• Mrs. Garland has 26 students in her fourth-grade class.
  She bought 156 pieces of saltwater taffy to share with her students.

  How much money did she spend? $_____

  How many pieces of taffy will each student get? _____

• Lewis bought 3 things. He spent $10.00 What did Lewis buy?

  _____

• Janie also bought 3 things. She spent $8.25. What did Janie buy?

  _____

• Coach Donovan bought a small bag of caramel corn for each of the
  14 players on his soccer team. How much money did the coach spend? $_____

• You have $9.00. What will you buy at Sandy's Candy?

  _____

  How much money did you spend? $_____

  How much change will you get back? $_____

Name _____

Rules

What are 3 rules for your school?

1. _____

2. _____

3. _____

What are 3 different rules for your house?

1. _____

2. _____

3. _____

Use the clues to find the words. Each word rhymes with this word:

RULE

use to fix things _____

swim here _____

chilly _____

holds thread _____

sit on this _____

unkind _____

silly person _____

place to learn _____

When Myron plays board games, he follows the rules only one-third of the time. He has played Monopoly 51 times. How many times has Myron <u>not</u> played by the rules?

_____ times

Do you always play by the rules? _____

Why or why not?

_____

_____

_____

_____

Rules

If you could make 3 rules that everyone on Earth would have to follow, what would they be?

1. _____

2. _____

3. _____

Use the clues to find things that have rules.

red and black squares   C_____

place with books   L_____

place you swim   P_____

plan for eating   D_____

summer activity place   C_____

on TV   G_____ S_____

word competition   S_____ B_____

At Stephen's house, there is a rule that he can watch only 7 hours of TV a week. Last week, he watched 3 half-hour sitcoms, 1 movie that was two hours long, a football game that lasted two and a half hours, and a half hour of cartoons. Did Stephen follow the rule?

_____

Do you think that kids should have TV limits?

_____

What does it mean to "bend the rules"?

_____

What is an example of someone bending the rules?

_____

_____

Do you ever bend the rules? _____

Rules

Think about the rules for tic-tac-toe. How can you change the rules to make the game more interesting? You can change anything about the game, even the way the grid looks.

Write your new rules.

_____

_____

_____

Draw your new game. If you changed the grid, be sure to draw it that way.

Try your new game with a friend, and then write what it was like.

_____

Do you like the original game of tic-tac-toe or your version better?

_____

Why? _____

_____

_____

_____

What are 3 other games that might be better if you changed the rules?

1. _____

2. _____

3. _____

   Critical and Creative Thinking Activities • EMC 3394 • © Evan-Moor Corp.

Answer Key

Many of the questions in this book are open-ended, and students' answers will vary. Sample responses are provided for most of these activities. Accept any reasonable responses.

Page 5

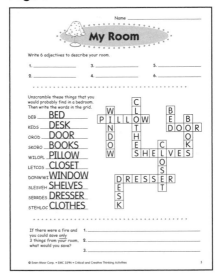

Page 6

My Room

Some kids share a room with a brother or a sister. Write 3 advantages and 3 disadvantages of sharing a room.

Advantages	Disadvantages

ANALOGIES

shelves : books :: closet : __clothes__
desk : study :: bed : __sleep__
posters : wall :: rug : __floor__
pillow : soft :: desk : __hard__

If these things could talk, what would they say?

Your floor: _____
Your closet: _____
Your alarm clock: _____
Your pillow: _____

Rate your room.

messy	1	2	3	4	5	neat
boring	1	2	3	4	5	interesting
uncomfortable	1	2	3	4	5	comfortable

Page 7

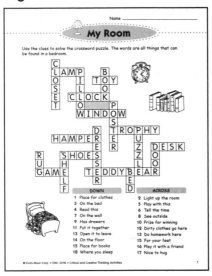

Page 8

Page 9

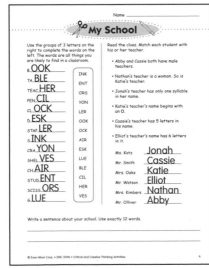

Page 10

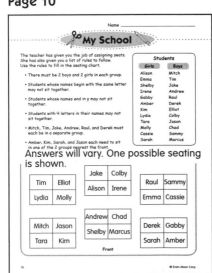

The Supermarket

Name _____

Write a sentence that is always true about the supermarket.

_____

Write a sentence that is sometimes true about the supermarket.

_____

Write a sentence that is never true about the supermarket.

_____

You get to do the grocery shopping! The only rule is that you must buy one thing from each of the sections listed below. What do you buy?

Dairy _____
Cereal _____
Produce _____
Beverages _____
Cookies _____
Meat _____
Freezer _____
Chips _____
Bakery _____

Circle the better deal each time.

Apples
(3 for $1.00) or 5 for $1.75

Toilet paper
3 rolls for $1.50 or (12 rolls for $5.25)

Candy bars
4 for $1.50 or (6 for $2.00)

Why do you think stores often have candy and gum at the checkout stand?

_____

© Evan-Moor Corp. • EMC 3394 • Critical and Creative Thinking Activities   11

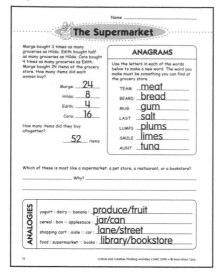

The Supermarket

Name _____

Marge bought 3 times as many groceries as Hilda. Edith bought half as many groceries as Hilda. Cora bought 4 times as many groceries as Edith. Marge bought 24 items at the grocery store. How many items did each woman buy?

Marge: **24**
Hilda: **8**
Edith: **4**
Cora: **16**

How many items did they buy altogether?

52 items

ANAGRAMS

Use the letters in each of the words below to make a new word. The word you make must be something you can find at the grocery store.

TEAM — **meat**
BEARD — **bread**
MUG — **gum**
LAST — **salt**
LUMPS — **plums**
SMILE — **limes**
AUNT — **tuna**

Which of these is most like a supermarket: a pet store, a restaurant, or a bookstore?

_____ Why? _____

ANALOGIES

yogurt : dairy :: banana : **produce/fruit**
cereal : box :: applesauce : **jar/can**
shopping cart : aisle :: car : **lane/street**
food : supermarket :: books : **library/bookstore**

12   Critical and Creative Thinking Activities • EMC 3394 • © Evan-Moor Corp.

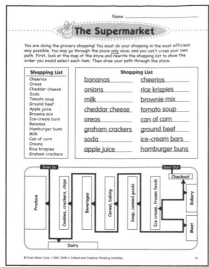

The Supermarket

Name _____

You are doing the grocery shopping! You must do your shopping in the most efficient way possible. You may go through the store only once, and you can't cross your own path. First, look at the map of the store and rewrite the shopping list to show the order you would select each item. Then draw your path through the store.

Shopping List
Cheerios
Oreos
Cheddar cheese
Soda
Tomato soup
Ground beef
Apple juice
Brownie mix
Ice-cream bars
Bananas
Hamburger buns
Milk
Can of corn
Onions
Rice krispies
Graham crackers

Shopping List
bananas   cheerios
onions   rice krispies
milk   brownie mix
cheddar cheese   tomato soup
oreos   can of corn
graham crackers ground beef
soda   ice-cream bars
apple juice   hamburger buns

© Evan-Moor Corp. • EMC 3394 • Critical and Creative Thinking Activities   13

At the Dinner Table

Name _____

Think about the table where you usually eat dinner.

What shape is it? _____ How many legs does it have? _____

What is it made out of? _____

When you sit at your usual spot at the table, what do you see...

straight ahead? _____

to the left? _____

to the right? _____

Where does each person sit? Label the chairs.

• Mom sits at the west end of the table, and Dad sits at the east end of the table.
• The twins, Lily and Susie, sit across from each other.
• Grandma sits to the left of Dad.
• Ben sits next to Susie.
• Lily sits to the right of Mom.

Susie Ben
Mom   Dad
Lily Grandma

Dinnertime is a good time to catch up with your family. What are 3 questions you could ask to make dinnertime more interesting?

1. _____
2. _____
3. _____

14   Critical and Creative Thinking Activities • EMC 3394 • © Evan-Moor Corp.

At the Dinner Table

Name _____

Dad made baked potatoes. If he puts 1 potato on everyone's plate, he will have one extra potato. If he puts 2 potatoes on everyone's plate, one person will not get any potatoes at all. How many people are in Dad's family, and how many baked potatoes did he make?

3 people
4 potatoes

Julia's family eats rice with dinner every third night. They have peas every fourth night. It is Monday night and Julia's family is eating both rice and peas. On what day of the week will they next eat rice and peas in the same meal?

Saturday

What are 5 other things you could use the dinner table for besides eating?

1. _____
2. _____
3. _____
4. _____
5. _____

Create the most disgusting dinner that you can imagine.

Main dish: _____
Side dish: _____
Vegetable: _____
Beverage: _____

Would you eat the dinner that you created for $100?

What is the most disgusting thing that you have ever eaten?

© Evan-Moor Corp. • EMC 3394 • Critical and Creative Thinking Activities   15

At the Dinner Table

Name _____

It's Rainbow Week at the Smith house! During Rainbow Week, the family eats a different color meal each night. Each meal must contain a main dish, a side dish, a vegetable, and a beverage. Every item must be the correct color. Can you think of a menu for each night?

	Main Dish	Side Dish	Vegetable	Beverage
Monday yellow				
Tuesday red				
Wednesday green				
Thursday brown				
Friday orange				
Saturday white				
Sunday purple				

Which night's dinner menu is your favorite? _____

Would you want to have Rainbow Week at your house? _____

Why or why not? _____

16   Critical and Creative Thinking Activities • EMC 3394 • © Evan-Moor Corp.

Eating Out

Name _____

What are 5 things that you can do to entertain yourself while you are waiting for the food to be served at a restaurant?

1. _____
2. _____
3. _____
4. _____
5. _____

Which restaurants do you like? Number them from 1 to 9. The one you like the most should be number 1.

___ Burrito Barn
___ Show Me the Sushi
___ Forever Fish
___ Penelope's Pancake Place
___ Burgers R Us
___ Spaghetti Already
___ Terrific Teriyaki
___ Souper Soup Shack
___ Pizza Palace

Maryann and Ginger went out for lunch. How much did each person spend?

Maryann
House salad $3.25
Chicken sandwich $6.70
Iced tea $2.15
Total: $ **12.10**

Ginger
Tomato soup $3.75
Grilled cheese $5.85
Soda $2.25
Total: $ **11.85**

How much did they spend altogether?
$ **23.95**

© Evan-Moor Corp. • EMC 3394 • Critical and Creative Thinking Activities   17

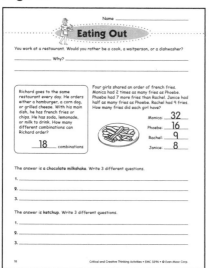

Eating Out

Name _____

You work at a restaurant. Would you rather be a cook, a waitperson, or a dishwasher?

_____ Why? _____

Richard goes to the same restaurant every day. He orders either a hamburger, a corn dog, or grilled cheese. With his main dish, he has french fries or chips. He has soda, lemonade, or milk to drink. How many different combinations can Richard order?

18 combinations

Four girls shared an order of french fries. Monica had 2 times as many fries as Phoebe. Phoebe had 7 more fries than Rachel. Janice had half as many fries as Phoebe. Rachel had 9 fries. How many fries did each girl have?

Monica: **32**
Phoebe: **16**
Rachel: **9**
Janice: **8**

The answer is a chocolate milkshake. Write 3 different questions.

1. _____
2. _____
3. _____

The answer is ketchup. Write 3 different questions.

1. _____
2. _____
3. _____

18   Critical and Creative Thinking Activities • EMC 3394 • © Evan-Moor Corp.

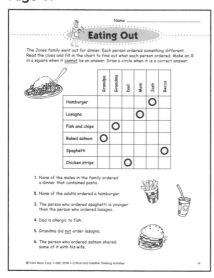

Eating Out

Name _____

The Jones family went out for dinner. Each person ordered something different. Read the clues and fill in the chart to find out what each person ordered. Make an X in a square when it cannot be an answer. Draw a circle in it when it is a correct answer.

	Grandpa	Grandma	Dad	Mom	Josh	Becca
Hamburger				○		
Lasagna					○	
Fish and chips		○				
Baked salmon	○					
Spaghetti						○
Chicken strips			○			

1. None of the males in the family ordered a dinner that contained pasta.
2. None of the adults ordered a hamburger.
3. The person who ordered spaghetti is younger than the person who ordered lasagna.
4. Dad is allergic to fish.
5. Grandma did not order lasagna.
6. The person who ordered salmon shared some of it with his wife.

© Evan-Moor Corp. • EMC 3394 • Critical and Creative Thinking Activities   19

Page 20

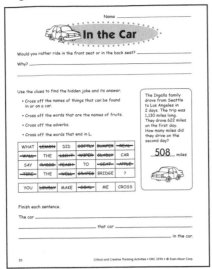

Name _____

In the Car

Would you rather ride in the front seat or in the back seat? _____
Why? _____

Use the clues to find the hidden joke and its answer.
- Cross off the names of things that can be found in or on a car.
- Cross off the words that are the names of fruits.
- Cross off the adverbs.
- Cross off the words that end in L.

WHAT	~~LEMON~~	DID	~~SOFTLY~~	~~BUMPER~~	~~REAL~~
~~WILL~~	THE	~~LIGHT~~	~~WIPER~~	~~GLADLY~~	CAR
SAY	~~RADIO~~	~~PEACH~~	TO	~~SEAT~~	~~APPLE~~
~~TIRE~~	THE	~~WELL~~	~~GRAPES~~	BRIDGE	?
YOU	~~LOUDLY~~	MAKE	~~GOAL~~	ME	CROSS

The Ingalls family drove from Seattle to Los Angeles in 2 days. The trip was 1,130 miles long. They drove 622 miles on the first day. How many miles did they drive on the second day?

508 miles

Finish each sentence.
The car _____ that car _____ _____ in the car.

Page 21

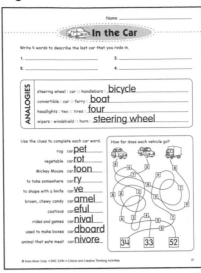

Name _____

In the Car

Write 4 words to describe the last car that you rode in.
1. _____ 3. _____
2. _____ 4. _____

ANALOGIES
steering wheel : car :: handlebars : **bicycle**
convertible : car :: ferry : **boat**
headlights : two :: tires : **four**
wipers : windshield :: horn : **steering wheel**

Use the clues to complete each car word.
rug — car **pet**
vegetable — car **rot**
Mickey Mouse — car **toon**
to take somewhere — car **ry**
to shape with a knife — car **ve**
brown, chewy candy — car **amel**
cautious — car **eful**
rides and games — car **nival**
used to make boxes — car **dboard**
animal that eats meat — car **nivore**

How far does each vehicle go?

34 **33** **52**

Page 22

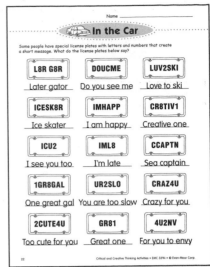

Name _____

In the Car

Some people have special license plates with letters and numbers that create a short message. What do the license plates below say?

L8R G8R — Later gator
DOUCME — Do you see me
LUV2SKI — Love to ski

ICESK8R — Ice skater
IMHAPP — I am happy
CR8TIV1 — Creative one

ICU2 — I see you too
IML8 — I'm late
CCAPTN — Sea captain

1GR8GAL — One great gal
UR2SLO — You are too slow
CRAZ4U — Crazy for you

2CUTE4U — Too cute for you
GR81 — Great one
4U2NV — For you to envy

Page 23

Name _____

On a Walk

Miles always takes the same path home from school. What are 3 reasons he might choose to walk home a different way?
1. _____
2. _____
3. _____

Think about the things that you might see on a walk in the country and in the city. Then fill in the chart. For each row, you must write words that begin with the letter you see on the left.

	In the Country	In the City
T		
C		
S		
F		
B		

Make each sentence more interesting by changing the verb and adding adjectives and adverbs.
The girl walked down the street.
_____
The man walked to the post office to mail the letter.
_____

Page 24

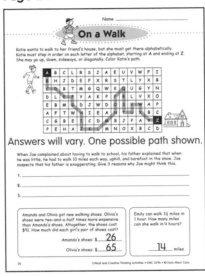

Name _____

On a Walk

Katie wants to walk to her friend's house, but she must get there alphabetically. Katie must step in order on each letter of the alphabet, starting at A and ending at Z. She may go up, down, sideways, or diagonally. Color Katie's path.

Answers will vary. One possible path shown.

When Joe complained about having to walk to school, his father explained that when he was little, he had to walk 10 miles each way, uphill, and barefoot in the snow. Joe suspects that his father is exaggerating. Give 3 reasons why Joe might think this.
1. _____
2. _____
3. _____

Amanda and Olivia got new walking shoes. Olivia's shoes were two-and-a-half times more expensive than Amanda's shoes. Altogether, the shoes cost $91. How much did each girl's pair of shoes cost?
Amanda's shoes: $ **26**
Olivia's shoes: $ **65**

Emily can walk 3½ miles in 1 hour. How many miles can she walk in 4 hours?
14 miles

Page 25

Name _____

On a Walk

Four children walked to the park. Each child followed a different set of directions. Color each child's path with a different color.

Eric
Kylie
Park
Carlos
Emily

Eric	Kylie	Carlos	Emily
5 blocks East	2 blocks East	1 block East	9 blocks East
3 blocks South	4 blocks North	4 blocks South	4 blocks North
6 blocks East	2 blocks East	2 blocks East	3 blocks East
2 blocks North	5 blocks South	2 blocks North	3 blocks South
4 blocks East	2 blocks East	2 blocks East	5 blocks South
4 blocks South	3 blocks North	3 blocks North	6 blocks East
	3 blocks North	8 blocks East	5 blocks North
	1 block South	1 block North	2 blocks West
	2 blocks East		2 blocks North

Page 26

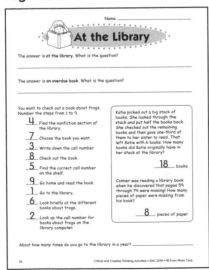

Name _____

At the Library

The answer is at the library. What is the question?
_____
The answer is an overdue book. What is the question?
_____

You want to check out a big stack of books. Number the steps from 1 to 9.
4 Find the nonfiction section of the library.
7 Choose the book you want.
3 Write down the call number.
8 Check out the book.
5 Find the correct call number on the shelf.
9 Go home and read the book.
1 Go to the library.
6 Look briefly at the different books about frogs.
2 Look up the call number for books about frogs on the library computer.

Katie picked out a big stack of books. She looked through the stack and put half the books back. She checked out the remaining books and then gave one-third of them to her sister to read. That left Katie with 6 books. How many books did Katie originally have in her stack at the library?
18 books

Connor was reading a library book when he discovered that pages 59 through 74 were missing! How many pieces of paper were missing from his book?
8 pieces of paper

About how many times do you go to the library in a year? _____

Page 27

Name _____

At the Library

Fill in the Venn diagram with at least 3 things in each section.

Library   Bookstore
Both

There are some things you can't do at the library. Why can't you...
talk loudly? _____
eat? _____
run? _____
take books without checking them out? _____

Alan checked out 23 books from the library. He returned them 6 days late. The fine is 10¢ a day per book. How much will Alan need to pay?
$ **13.80**

Alan paid his fine with a twenty-dollar bill. How much change will he get back?
$ **6.20**

Page 28

Name _____

At the Library

The library books below were all written by authors with names that go with what they wrote about. Use the numbers to match the books with their authors.

1. How to Pay Off Your Debts
2. Karaoke for Everyone!
3. Finding Buried Treasure
4. Into the Haunted House
5. Run Your Own Gas Station
6. Celebrity Lives
7. Climbing Mount Everest
8. At the Library
9. Fix Your Roof
10. First Aid for Beginners
11. Goodbye, My Love
12. Come Inside

9 Lee King
2 Carrie A. Toon
5 Phil R. Up
7 Will E. Maykit

1 Owen Kash
11 C.U. Later
10 Justin Case
12 Doris Open

4 Hugo Furst
3 Doug A. Whole
8 Rita Book
6 Rich N. Famous

Page 29

Name _____

At the Beach

What is your favorite thing to do at the beach?
_____

What would be a silly thing to do at the beach?
_____

What can you find at the beach that begins with each letter? | You are going to the beach. What are the 4 most important things to take with you?
S _____ | 1. _____
T _____ | 2. _____
W _____ | 3. _____
D _____ | 4. _____
C _____ |

The answer is at the beach. What is the question?
_____

The answer is a really big wave. What is the question?
_____

What do they say?

sea gull | Lifeguard Duty — lifeguard on duty | TIDE — high tide

© Evan-Moor Corp. 29

Page 30

Name _____

At the Beach

Write a sentence that is always true about the beach.
_____

Write a sentence that is sometimes true about the beach.
_____

Write a sentence that is never true about the beach.
_____

Pamela went to the beach. She swam in the water before she ate lunch. She ate lunch before she made a sand castle. She made a sand castle after she got ice cream. Write what Pamela did in the correct order.

First: swam
Second: ate lunch
Third: got ice cream
Fourth: made a sand castle

There is a lot of sand at the beach! Number the places where you might find sand from 1 to 6. The worst place should be number 1.

____ in your sandwich
____ on your towel
____ under your swimsuit
____ in your hair
____ on your ice cream
____ in your eyes

Add 2 more words to the list, and then tell how the words are all related.
sea star, crab, clam, any animals in the ocean

towel, bucket, sunscreen, any items one might take to the beach

30   Critical and Creative Thinking Activities • EMC 3394 • © Evan-Moor Corp.

Page 31

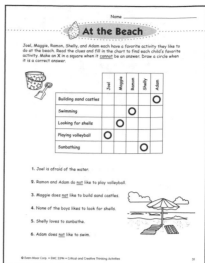

Name _____

At the Beach

Joel, Maggie, Ramon, Shelly, and Adam each have a favorite activity they like to do at the beach. Read the clues and fill in the chart to find each child's favorite activity. Make an X in a square when it cannot be an answer. Draw a circle when it is a correct answer.

	Joel	Maggie	Ramon	Shelly	Adam
Building sand castles					O
Swimming			O		
Looking for shells			O		
Playing volleyball	O				
Sunbathing					O

1. Joel is afraid of the water.
2. Ramon and Adam do not like to play volleyball.
3. Maggie does not like to build sand castles.
4. None of the boys likes to look for shells.
5. Shelly loves to sunbathe.
6. Adam does not like to swim.

© Evan-Moor Corp. • EMC 3394 • Critical and Creative Thinking Activities 31

Page 32

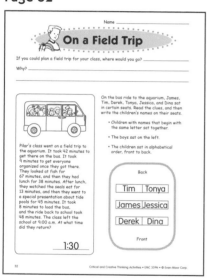

Name _____

On a Field Trip

If you could plan a field trip for your class, where would you go? _____
Why? _____

On the bus ride to the aquarium, James, Tim, Derek, Tonya, Jessica, and Dina sat in certain seats. Read the clues, and then write the children's names on their seats.

• Children with names that begin with the same letter sat together.
• The boys sat on the left.
• The children sat in alphabetical order, front to back.

Pilar's class went on a field trip to the aquarium. It took 42 minutes to get them on the bus. It took 9 minutes to get everyone organized once they got there. They looked at fish for 67 minutes, and then they had lunch for 38 minutes. After lunch, they watched the seals eat for 13 minutes, and then they went to a special presentation about tide pools for 45 minutes. It took 8 minutes to load the bus, and the ride back to school took 48 minutes. The bus left the school at 9:00 a.m. At what time did they return?

1:30

Back
Tim | Tonya
James | Jessica
Derek | Dina
Front

32   Critical and Creative Thinking Activities • EMC 3394 • © Evan-Moor Corp.

Page 33

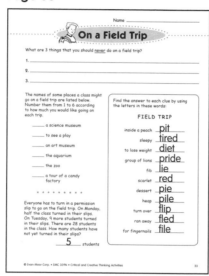

Name _____

On a Field Trip

What are 3 things that you should never do on a field trip?
1. _____
2. _____
3. _____

The names of some places a class might go on a field trip are listed below. Number them from 1 to 6 according to how much you would like going on each trip.

____ a science museum
____ to see a play
____ an art museum
____ the aquarium
____ the zoo
____ a tour of a candy factory

Everyone has to turn in a permission slip to go on the field trip. On Monday, half the class turned in their slips. On Tuesday, 9 more students turned in their slips. There are 28 students in the class. How many students have not yet turned in their slips?

____5____ students

Find the answer to each clue by using the letters in these words:

FIELD TRIP

inside a peach — pit
sleepy — tired
to lose weight — diet
group of lions — pride
fib — lie
scarlet — red
dessert — pie
heap — pile
turn over — flip
ran away — fled
for fingernails — file

© Evan-Moor Corp. • EMC 3394 • Critical and Creative Thinking Activities 33

Page 34

Name _____

On a Field Trip

Ryan has gotten separated from his class on the field trip. He needs to make it back to the bus before it leaves. To help Ryan get back to the bus, start at the square in the upper-left corner. Move the same number of squares as the number shown (2). Move in a straight line in any direction. When you get to the next square, move the same number of squares as the number shown. Can you make a path that will take Ryan to the bus? Color the path.

Answers will vary.
One possible path is shown.

2	7	3	6	1	5	9	2	1	8	4	3
5	2	2	6	3	1	9	5	2	6	6	2
7	8	1	6	2	7	1	5	2	6	6	2
1	3	4	2	7	2	4	4	7	1	1	7
2	7	3	6	1	3	9	2	1	8	4	3
1	3	4	2	7	2	4	4	7	1	1	7
5	2	2	6	3	1	3	7	5	2	9	1
7	8	1	6	2	4	3	2	4	4	6	2
2	7	3	6	1	4	9	2	1	2	4	6
1	3	4	2	7	2	3	8	4	3	6	1
7	8	1	6	2	1	1	4	2	6	6	1
5	2	2	8	3	1	3	5	3	2	3	1

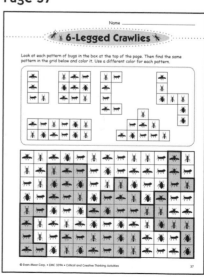

34   Critical and Creative Thinking Activities • EMC 3394 • © Evan-Moor Corp.

Page 35

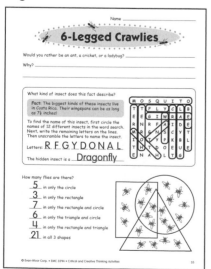

Name _____

6-Legged Crawlies

Would you rather be an ant, a cricket, or a ladybug? _____
Why? _____

What kind of insect does this fact describe?

Fact: The biggest kinds of these insects live in Costa Rica. Their wingspans can be as long as 7½ inches.

To find the name of this insect, first circle the names of 12 different insects in the word search. Next, write the remaining letters on the lines. Then unscramble the letters to name the insect.

M O S Q U I T O
T T F L Y C L B
E E G I W R A E
R N R F A I D E
M S N S C Y T T
I T U T D O K L
T A N H L U T E

Letters: R F G Y D O N A L
The hidden insect is a Dragonfly

How many flies are there?
5 in only the circle
3 in only the rectangle
7 in the rectangle and circle
6 in the triangle and circle
4 in the rectangle and triangle
21 in all 3 shapes

© Evan-Moor Corp. • EMC 3394 • Critical and Creative Thinking Activities 35

Page 36

Name _____

6-Legged Crawlies

Are you afraid of bugs? _____ Why or why not? _____

Fill in the missing vowels.

A n t
M O t h
c r i c k E t
h O U s E f l y
l A d y b U g
b E E t l E
g r A s s h O p p E r
m O s q u i t O
p r A y i n g m A n t i s
s t i n k b U g
c O c k r O A c h

Tamara was catching ladybugs to put in her garden. She caught 17 ladybugs on Wednesday. She caught a total of 41 ladybugs on Thursday and Friday. She caught a total of 33 ladybugs on Wednesday and Thursday. How many ladybugs did Tamara catch on each day?

Wednesday: 17
Thursday: 24
Friday: 9

How many bugs did she catch on all 3 days?
50

ANALOGIES
beetle : insect :: lizard : reptile
cricket : green :: ladybug : red
ant : hill :: bee : hive
insect : six :: spider : eight

36   Critical and Creative Thinking Activities • EMC 3394 • © Evan-Moor Corp.

Page 37

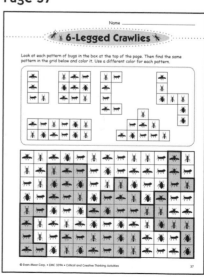

Name _____

6-Legged Crawlies

Look at each pattern of bugs in the box at the top of the page. Then find the same pattern in the grid below and color it. Use a different color for each pattern.

© Evan-Moor Corp. • EMC 3394 • Critical and Creative Thinking Activities 37

Critical and Creative Thinking Activities • EMC 3394 • © Evan-Moor Corp.

Page 38

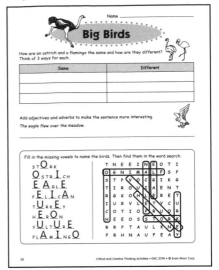

Big Birds

How are an ostrich and a flamingo the same and how are they different? Think of 3 ways for each.

Same	Different

Add adjectives and adverbs to make the sentence more interesting.

The eagle flew over the meadow.

_____

Fill in the missing vowels to name the birds. Then find them in the word search.

```
STORK
OSTRICH
EAGLE
PELICAN
TURKEY
HERON
VULTURE
FLAMINGO
```

```
T N E E I N E O T I
O G N I M A L F S P
S T P V O C G I K G
T I R O U T A E N T
R G K O H L E R E T
I U R V L E T Y C U
C O T I O R U R O R
H E E O S T O R K E
R R P T A U L K N E
P R H N A U F E A Y
```

Page 39

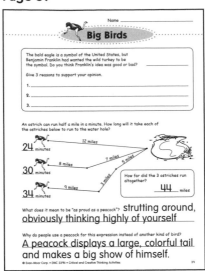

Big Birds

The bald eagle is a symbol of the United States, but Benjamin Franklin had wanted the wild turkey to be the symbol. Do you think Franklin's idea was good or bad?

Give 3 reasons to support your opinion.

1. _____
2. _____
3. _____

An ostrich can run half a mile in a minute. How long will it take each of the ostriches below to run to the water hole?

24 minutes — 12 miles

30 minutes — 8 miles — 7 miles

34 minutes — 9 miles

How far did the 3 ostriches run altogether? **44** miles

What does it mean to be "as proud as a peacock"? **strutting around, obviously thinking highly of yourself**

Why do people use a peacock for this expression instead of another kind of bird? **A peacock displays a large, colorful tail and makes a big show of himself.**

Page 40

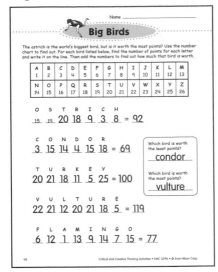

Big Birds

The ostrich is the world's biggest bird, but is it worth the most points? Use the number chart to find out. For each bird listed below, find the number of points for each letter and write it on the line. Then add the numbers to find out how much that bird is worth.

A	B	C	D	E	F	G	H	I	J	K	L	M
1	2	3	4	5	6	7	8	9	10	11	12	13

N	O	P	Q	R	S	T	U	V	W	X	Y	Z
14	15	16	17	18	19	20	21	22	23	24	25	26

O S T R I C H
15 19 20 18 9 3 8 = 92

C O N D O R
3 15 14 4 15 18 = 69

Which bird is worth the least points? **condor**

T U R K E Y
20 21 18 11 5 25 = 100

Which bird is worth the most points? **vulture**

V U L T U R E
22 21 12 20 21 18 5 = 119

F L A M I N G O
6 12 1 13 9 14 7 15 = 77

Page 41

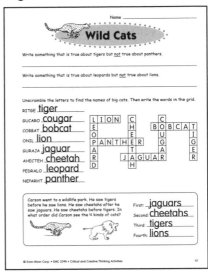

Wild Cats

Write something that is true about tigers but not true about panthers.

_____

Write something that is true about leopards but not true about lions.

_____

Unscramble the letters to find the names of big cats. Then write the words in the grid.

RITGE — **tiger**
GUCARO — **cougar**
COBBAT — **bobcat**
ONIL — **lion**
GURAJA — **jaguar**
AHECTEH — **cheetah**
PEDRALO — **leopard**
NEPARHT — **panther**

```
  L I O N   C
  E       H   B O B C A T
O P A N T H E R       I
  A       E   U       G
  R       T   G       E
  D       A   A       R
    J A G U A R
        H
```

Carson went to a wildlife park. He saw tigers before he saw lions. He saw cheetahs after he saw jaguars. He saw cheetahs before tigers. In what order did Carson see the 4 kinds of cats?

First: **jaguars**
Second: **cheetahs**
Third: **tigers**
Fourth: **lions**

Page 42

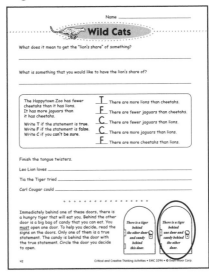

Wild Cats

What does it mean to get the "lion's share" of something?

_____

What is something that you would like to have the lion's share of?

_____

The Happytown Zoo has fewer cheetahs than it has lions. It has more jaguars than it has cheetahs.

Write T if the statement is true.
Write F if the statement is false.
Write C if you can't be sure.

T There are more lions than cheetahs.
F There are fewer jaguars than cheetahs.
C There are fewer jaguars than lions.
C There are more jaguars than lions.
F There are more cheetahs than lions.

Finish the tongue twisters.

Leo Lion loves _____

Tia the Tiger tried _____

Carl Cougar could _____

Immediately behind one of these doors, there is a hungry tiger that will eat you. Behind the other door is a big bag of candy that you can eat. You must open one door. To help you decide, read the signs on the doors. Only one of them is a true statement. The candy is behind the door with the true statement. Circle the door you decide to open.

There is a tiger behind the other door and candy behind this door.

There is a tiger behind one door and candy behind the other door.

Page 43

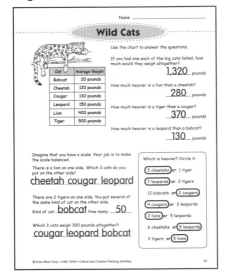

Wild Cats

Use the chart to answer the questions.

Cat	Average Weight
Bobcat	20 pounds
Cheetah	120 pounds
Cougar	130 pounds
Leopard	150 pounds
Lion	400 pounds
Tiger	500 pounds

If you had one each of the big cats listed, how much would they weigh altogether? **1,320** pounds

How much heavier is a lion than a cheetah? **280** pounds

How much heavier is a tiger than a cougar? **370** pounds

How much heavier is a leopard than a bobcat? **130** pounds

Imagine that you have a scale. Your job is to make the scale balanced.

There is a lion on one side. Which 3 cats do you put on the other side? **cheetah cougar leopard**

There are 2 tigers on one side. You put several of the same kind of cat on the other side.
Kind of cat: **bobcat** How many: **50**

Which 3 cats weigh 300 pounds altogether? **cougar leopard bobcat**

Which is heavier? Circle it.
(5 cheetahs) or 1 tiger
(7 leopards) or 2 tigers
12 bobcats or (2 cougars)
(4 cougars) or 3 leopards
(2 lions) or 5 leopards
6 cheetahs or (5 leopards)
3 tigers or (5 lions)

Page 44

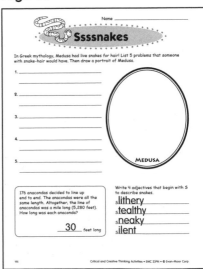

Sssssnakes

In Greek mythology, Medusa had live snakes for hair! List 5 problems that someone with snake-hair would have. Then draw a portrait of Medusa.

1. _____
2. _____
3. _____
4. _____
5. _____

MEDUSA

176 anacondas decided to line up end to end. The anacondas were all the same length. Altogether, the line of anacondas was a mile long (5,280 feet). How long was each anaconda? **30** feet long

Write 4 adjectives that begin with S to describe snakes.
S**lithery**
S**tealthy**
S**neaky**
S**ilent**

Page 45

Ssssnakes

There are nearly 3,000 kinds of snakes. How many kinds can you name?

1. _____ 5. _____
2. _____ 6. _____
3. _____ 7. _____
4. _____ 8. _____

Sally Snake is longer than Susie Snake. Sammy Snake is longer than Sally Snake. Simon Snake is shorter than Susie Snake. Put the 4 snakes in order from longest to shortest.

Sammy
Sally
Susie
Simon

Jake the Snake is a yard and a foot plus an inch long. How long is Jake the Snake in inches? **49** inches long

Blake the Snake is one-eighth of two yards long. How many inches long is Blake the Snake? **9** inches long

Compose a short rhyming poem using the words snake, bake, cake, and lake.

_____

Illustrate your poem.

Page 46

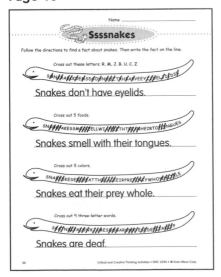

Ssssnakes

Follow the directions to find a fact about snakes. Then write the fact on the line.

Cross out these letters: R, M, J, B, U, C, Z

Snakes don't have eyelids.

Cross out 5 foods.

Snakes smell with their tongues.

Cross out 5 colors.

Snakes eat their prey whole.

Cross out 9 three-letter words.

Snakes are deaf.

Page 47

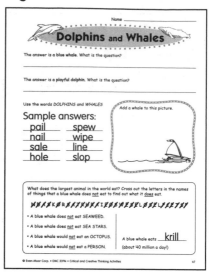

Dolphins and Whales

Name _____

The answer is a blue whale. What is the question?

_____

The answer is a playful dolphin. What is the question?

_____

Use the words *DOLPHINS* and *WHALES*

Sample answers:

pail	spew
nail	wipe
sale	line
hole	slop

Add a whale to this picture.

What does the largest animal in the world eat? Cross out the letters in the names of things that a blue whale does <u>not</u> eat to find out what it <u>does</u> eat.

~~W~~ ~~K~~ ~~S~~ ~~E~~ ~~A~~ ~~W~~ ~~R~~ ~~E~~ ~~A~~ ~~T~~ ~~S~~ ~~K~~ ~~R~~ ~~I~~ ~~L~~ ~~L~~ ~~E~~ ~~P~~ ~~E~~ ~~R~~ ~~S~~ ~~O~~ ~~L~~ ~~S~~ ~~E~~ ~~T~~ ~~Y~~

• A blue whale does <u>not</u> eat SEAWEED.

• A blue whale does <u>not</u> eat SEA STARS.

• A blue whale would <u>not</u> eat an OCTOPUS.

• A blue whale would <u>not</u> eat a PERSON.

A blue whale eats __krill__
(about 40 million a day!)

© Evan-Moor Corp. EMC 3394 • Critical and Creative Thinking Activities   47

Page 48

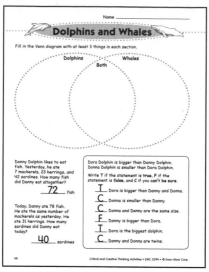

Dolphins and Whales

Name _____

Fill in the Venn diagram with at least 3 things in each section.

Dolphins   Whales

Both

Danny Dolphin likes to eat fish. Yesterday, he ate 7 mackerels, 23 herrings, and 42 sardines. How many fish did Danny eat altogether?

__72__ fish

Today, Danny ate 78 fish. He ate the same number of mackerels as yesterday. He ate 31 herrings. How many sardines did Danny eat today?

__40__ sardines

Dora Dolphin is bigger than Danny Dolphin. Donna Dolphin is smaller than Dora Dolphin.

Write T if the statement is **true**, F if the statement is **false**, and C if you can't be sure.

__T__ Dora is bigger than Danny and Donna.

__C__ Donna is smaller than Danny.

__C__ Donna and Danny are the same size.

__F__ Danny is bigger than Dora.

__T__ Dora is the biggest dolphin.

__C__ Danny and Donna are twins.

48   Critical and Creative Thinking Activities • EMC 3394 • © Evan-Moor Corp.

Page 49

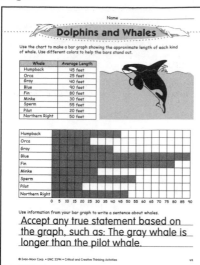

Dolphins and Whales

Name _____

Use the chart to make a bar graph showing the approximate length of each kind of whale. Use different colors to help the bars stand out.

Whale	Average Length
Humpback	45 feet
Orca	25 feet
Gray	40 feet
Blue	90 feet
Fin	80 feet
Minke	30 feet
Sperm	55 feet
Pilot	20 feet
Northern Right	50 feet

Humpback
Orca
Gray
Blue
Fin
Minke
Sperm
Pilot
Northern Right

0 5 10 15 20 25 30 35 40 45 50 55 60 65 70 75 80 85 90

Use information from your bar graph to write a sentence about whales.

Accept any true statement based on the graph, such as: The gray whale is longer than the pilot whale.

© Evan-Moor Corp. EMC 3394 • Critical and Creative Thinking Activities   49

Page 50

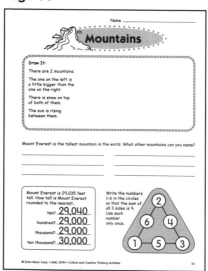

Trees

Name _____

Write 3 things that all trees have in common.

1. _____
2. _____
3. _____

The tree names below are missing their vowels. Fill in the letters, and then write the names of the trees in the grid.

E L M   D O g w O O d
F I r   H E M L O c k
O A k   R E d w O O d
P A L M
P I N E
B E E c h
B I r c h
c E d A r
m A P L E
w I L L O w

[crossword grid with: BELM, BEECH, WILLOW, BIRCH, PINE, REDWOOD, MAPLE, DOGWOOD, FIR, OAK, PALM, etc.]

Write a sentence about a tree. Use exactly 8 words.

_____

50   Critical and Creative Thinking Activities • EMC 3394 • © Evan-Moor Corp.

Page 51

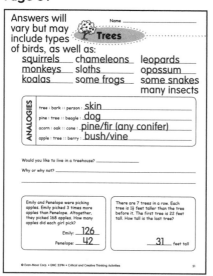

Trees

Name _____

Answers will vary but may include types of birds, as well as:

squirrels	chameleons	leopards
monkeys	sloths	opossum
koalas	some frogs	some snakes
		many insects

ANALOGIES

tree : bark :: person : __skin__

pine : tree :: beagle : __dog__

acorn : oak :: cone : __pine/fir (any conifer)__

apple : tree :: berry : __bush/vine__

Would you like to live in a treehouse? _____

Why or why not? _____

Emily and Penelope were picking apples. Emily picked 3 times more apples than Penelope. Altogether, they picked 168 apples. How many apples did each girl pick?

Emily: __126__

Penelope: __42__

There are 7 trees in a row. Each tree is 1½ feet taller than the tree before it. The first tree is 22 feet tall. How tall is the last tree?

__31__ feet tall

© Evan-Moor Corp. EMC 3394 • Critical and Creative Thinking Activities   51

Page 52

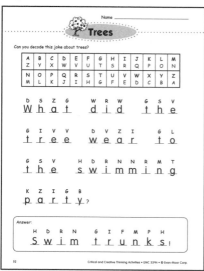

Trees

Name _____

Can you decode this joke about trees?

A	B	C	D	E	F	G	H	I	J	K	L	M
Z	Y	X	W	V	U	T	S	R	Q	P	O	N

N	O	P	Q	R	S	T	U	V	W	X	Y	Z
M	L	K	J	I	H	G	F	E	D	C	B	A

D S Z G   W R W   G S V
__What__ __did__ __the__

G I V V   D V Z I   G L
__tree__ __wear__ __to__

G S V   H D R N N R M T
__the__ __swimming__

K Z I G B
__party__?

Answer:
H D R N   G I F M P H
__Swim__ __trunks__!

52   Critical and Creative Thinking Activities • EMC 3394 • © Evan-Moor Corp.

Page 53

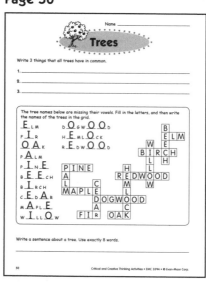

Mountains

Name _____

Draw it:

There are 2 mountains.

The one on the left is a little bigger than the one on the right.

There is snow on top of both of them.

The sun is rising between them.

Mount Everest is the tallest mountain in the world. What other mountains can you name?

_____

Mount Everest is 29,035 feet tall. How tall is Mount Everest rounded to the nearest...

ten? __29,040__

hundred? __29,000__

thousand? __29,000__

ten thousand? __30,000__

Write the numbers 1-6 in the circles so that the sum of all 3 sides is 9. Use each number only once.

[triangle with circles: 2, 4, 6, 1, 5, 3]

© Evan-Moor Corp. EMC 3394 • Critical and Creative Thinking Activities   53

Page 54

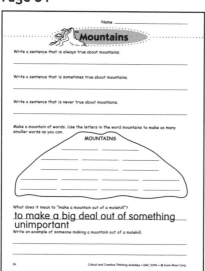

Mountains

Name _____

Write a sentence that is always true about mountains.

_____

Write a sentence that is sometimes true about mountains.

_____

Write a sentence that is never true about mountains.

_____

Make a mountain of words. Use the letters in the word mountains to make as many smaller words as you can.

MOUNTAINS

_____

What does it mean to "make a mountain out of a molehill"?

to make a big deal out of something unimportant

Write an example of someone making a mountain out of a molehill.

_____

54   Critical and Creative Thinking Activities • EMC 3394 • © Evan-Moor Corp.

Page 55

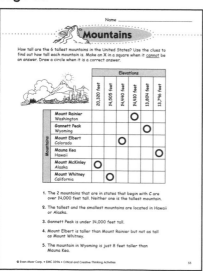

Mountains

Name _____

How tall are the 6 tallest mountains in the United States? Use the clues to find out how tall each mountain is. Make an X in a square when it *cannot* be an answer. Draw a circle when it is a correct answer.

	Elevations					
	20,320 feet	14,505 feet	14,440 feet	14,410 feet	13,804 feet	13,796 feet
Mount Rainier Washington				O		
Gannett Peak Wyoming					O	
Mount Elbert Colorado			O			
Mauna Kea Hawaii						O
Mount McKinley Alaska	O					
Mount Whitney California		O				

1. The 2 mountains that are in states that begin with C are over 14,000 feet tall. Neither one is the tallest mountain.

2. The tallest and the smallest mountains are located in Hawaii or Alaska.

3. Gannett Peak is under 14,000 feet tall.

4. Mount Elbert is taller than Mount Rainier but not as tall as Mount Whitney.

5. The mountain in Wyoming is just 8 feet taller than Mauna Kea.

© Evan-Moor Corp. EMC 3394 • Critical and Creative Thinking Activities   55

Page 56

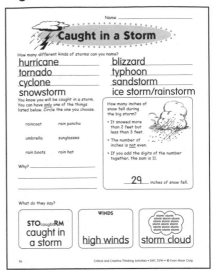

Caught in a Storm

How many different kinds of storms can you name?

hurricane / blizzard
tornado / typhoon
cyclone / sandstorm
snowstorm / ice storm/rainstorm

How many inches of snow fell during the big storm?

29 inches of snow fell.

What do they say?

STOcaughtRM — caught in a storm
WINDS — high winds
storm cloud

Page 57

Caught in a Storm

Unscramble the storm-related words.

LIHA	hail
DWIN	wind
WOSN	snow
NIRA	rain
SETLE	sleet
TEEWHAR	weather
SOLDUC	clouds
DREHUNT	thunder
ZADRIBZL	blizzard
DOONTAR	tornado
GGIINNHLT	lightning

Remaining letters: WSOENLARNE

The city that suffered a major hurricane is
New Orleans

Page 58

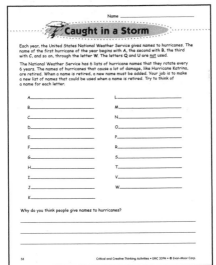

Caught in a Storm

Page 59

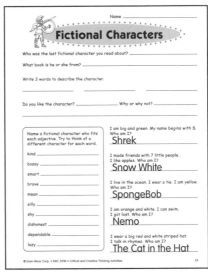

Fictional Characters

I am big and green. My name begins with S. Who am I?
Shrek

I made friends with 7 little people. I like apples. Who am I?
Snow White

I live in the ocean. I wear a tie. I am yellow. Who am I?
SpongeBob

I am orange and white. I can swim. I got lost. Who am I?
Nemo

I wear a big red and white striped hat. I talk in rhymes. Who am I?
The Cat in the Hat

Page 60

Fictional Characters

ANALOGIES

Shiloh : dog :: Charlotte : **spider**
Charlie Bucket : Roald Dahl :: Harry Potter : **J. K. Rowling**
Jack Spratt : nursery rhyme :: Cinderella : **fairy tale**

An Oompa-Loompa can make 258 Everlasting Gobstoppers in one hour. How many can he make in 36 hours?
9,288 Everlasting Gobstoppers

Peter Pan lives in Neverland, so he never grows up. If Peter was 9 years old when he got to Neverland in 1911 (when the book was published), how
Answer depends on current year.

Page 61

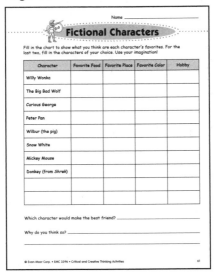

Fictional Characters

Page 62

Friends

Grace asked 27 of her friends what they like on their ice cream...
1 friend(s)

Ben and his dad went hiking with 6 friends...
3:00

How many people were on the hike?
8 people

Page 63

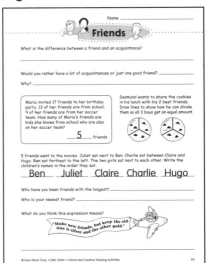

Friends

Maria invited 17 friends to her birthday party...
5 friends

Desmond wants to share the cookies...

5 friends went to the movies. Juliet sat next to Ben. Charlie sat between Claire and Hugo. Ben sat farthest to the left. The two girls sat next to each other. Write the children's names in the order they sat.
Ben   Juliet   Claire   Charlie   Hugo

Page 64

Friends

- Riding bikes   **Madison** and **Olivia**
- Baking cookies **Elly** and **Perry**
- Ice-skating   **Mandy** and **Sophie**
- Movies   **Jacob** and **Ethan**
- Mini golf   **Andy** and **Abby**
- Video games   **Michael** and **Matthew**
- Magic show   **Will** and **Isabel**
- Frisbee   **Daniel** and **Hannah**

Answers will vary. Possible combinations shown.

Page 65

Family Tree

Lester and Sadie had 4 children. Each of their children had 3 children. Each of those children had 2 children. How many great-grandchildren do Lester and Sadie have?

24

Your mother's father is your **grandfather**
Your father's sister is your **aunt**
Your grandmother's daughter is your **mother or aunt**
Your uncle's child is your **cousin**
Your father's grandfath **great grandfather**
Your grandfather's sister is your **great aunt**
Your sister's son would be your **nephew**

Being the oldest or the youngest or an only child has advantages and disadvantages. Fill in the chart to show at least one for each.

	Advantages	Disadvantages
Oldest		
Youngest		
Only child		

If you could choose, would you want to be the oldest, the youngest, or an only child? _____ Why? _____

Page 66

Family Tree

How many people are in your immediate family? _____

You are a son or a daughter. What other family roles do you have? _____

How many people are in your family, including grandparents, aunts, uncles, and cousins? _____

Write 5 words to describe your father.
1. _____
2. _____
3. _____
4. _____
5. _____

How are you the same as your father? _____

How are you different from your father? _____

Write 5 words to describe your mother.
1. _____
2. _____
3. _____
4. _____
5. _____

How are you the same as your mother? _____

How are you different from your mother? _____

Page 67

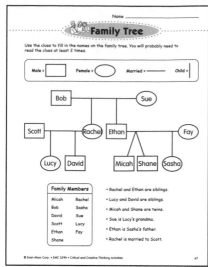

Family Tree

Use the clues to fill in the names on the family tree. You will probably need to read the clues at least 2 times.

Male = ☐   Female = ⬭   Married = ——   Child = |

Bob — Sue
Scott Rachel Ethan Fay
Lucy David Micah Shane Sasha

Family Members

Micah	Rachel
Bob	Sasha
David	Sue
Scott	Lucy
Ethan	Fay
Shane	

- Rachel and Ethan are siblings.
- Lucy and David are siblings.
- Micah and Shane are twins.
- Sue is Lucy's grandma.
- Ethan is Sasha's father.
- Rachel is married to Scott.

Page 68

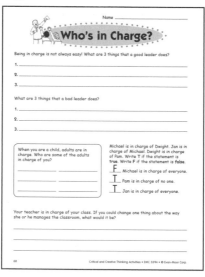

Who's in Charge?

Being in charge is not always easy! What are 3 things that a good leader does?
1. _____
2. _____
3. _____

What are 3 things that a bad leader does?
1. _____
2. _____
3. _____

When you are a child, adults are in charge of you. Who are some of the adults in charge of you?

Michael is in charge of Dwight. Jan is in charge of Michael. Dwight is in charge of Pam. Write T if the statement is true. Write F if the statement is false.

F Michael is in charge of everyone.
T Pam is in charge of no one.
T Jan is in charge of everyone.

Your teacher is in charge of your class. If you could change one thing about the way she or he manages the classroom, what would it be?

Page 69

Who's in Charge?

If you were in charge of your class for the next 15 minutes, what would you do? _____

Adults are not always in charge. They often have bosses or supervisors where they work. Who is in charge of the people listed below?

Teacher **principal**
Grocery checker **store mgr**
Football player **coach**
Actor **director**
Firefighter **fire captain**
Dental assistant **dentist**
Deputy **sheriff**
Author **publisher**

Carla is the president of a computer software company. She has 7 vice presidents. Each vice president has 4 managers. Each manager has 14 programmers.

How many programmers work for Carla's company?
392 programmers

How many people (including Carla) work at Carla's company altogether?
428 people

Who is in charge of the president of the United States? _____

Why do you think so? _____

Page 70

Who's in Charge?

Who owns the businesses listed below? Use the clues to find out. Make an X in a square when it cannot be an answer. Draw a circle when it is a correct answer.

	Mr. Appleton	Ms. Billings	Mr. Carlson	Mrs. Deets	Mr. Everett	Ms. Ford
Toilet Town				O		
Wrench Warehouse	O					
Mostly Mittens			O			
Paper Clip Palace						O
Exclusively Eggs		O				
The Fork Factory					O	

1. Mr. Carlson and Mrs. Deets do not own businesses that sell things that are made from metal.

2. Ms. Billings is dating the man who sells toilets. Her best friend is the woman who manufactures mittens.

3. Mr. Appleton does not sell paper clips or toilets.

4. The person who sells forks has been considering expanding her business to include spoons. But when she talked to Ms. Ford about it, Ms. Ford did not think it was such a good idea.

5. In order to get a jump on the competition, Mr. Carlson sells his product in a carton of 13 instead of the usual dozen.

Page 71

Superheroes

How many superheroes can you name? Use the back if you need more room.
1. _____ 5. _____
2. _____ 6. _____
3. _____ 7. _____
4. _____ 8. _____

Number the superpowers from 1 to 8. The one you think is best should be number 1.
___ super strength
___ invisibility
___ flight
___ shape shifting
___ super speed
___ X-ray vision
___ weather control
___ breathe underwater

Batman captured 11 bad guys on Tuesday. On Wednesday and Thursday, he captured a total of 23 bad guys. He captured a total of 18 bad guys on Tuesday and Wednesday. How many bad guys did Batman capture on each day?

Tuesday: **11**
Wednesday: **7**
Thursday: **16**

How many bad guys did Batman capture altogether?
34 bad guys

Write a sentence about a superhero. Use exactly 3 words.
_____

Write a sentence about a superhero. Use exactly 10 words.
_____

Page 72

Superheroes

If you could have one superpower, what would it be? _____

Why? _____

ANALOGIES

Spiderman : red :: The Incredible Hulk : **green**
Clark Kent : Superman :: Bruce Wayne : **Batman**
Wonder Woman : invisible plane :: Batman : **Batmobile**

How do you think our world might be different if superheroes really existed? _____

If superheroes did exist, would you want to be one? _____
Why or why not? _____

Superwoman has had a busy day. First, she flew 1,247 miles from her home in Metropolis to New York, where she saved a little girl from being run over by a taxi. Next, she sped 3,628 miles to Paris to keep an earthquake from tumbling the Eiffel Tower. After that, it was 8,493 miles to China, where she arrived just in time to catch a man who'd fallen off the Great Wall. Then she flew 4,586 miles to Australia to capture some escaped criminals. Finally, she flew 9,364 miles home to Metropolis. How many miles did Superwoman fly altogether?
27,318 miles

Page 73

Superheroes

Invent a superhero! First, answer the questions about your superhero. Then draw a picture of him or her. Your superhero can be serious or silly.

What is your superhero called? _____

What superpowers does he or she have? _____

How did your superhero get his or her superpowers? _____

What kinds of things does your superhero do to help people? _____

Page 74

Elves and Fairies

Elves and fairies are often in storybooks. What stories have you read or had read to you that included these kinds of characters?

1. _____ 4. _____
2. _____ 5. _____
3. _____ 6. _____

How do you think elves and fairies are the same?
_____

How do you think elves and fairies are different?
_____

Fairies love to frolic in the meadow. Yesterday, the fairies got up at dawn, which was at 5:43, and frolicked until dusk, which was at 9:24. How long did the fairies frolic?
15 hours **41** minutes

Elves have been known to make shoes for people during the night. If an elf can make a pair of shoes in half an hour, how many pairs of shoes can 3 elves make in 8 hours?
48 pairs of shoes

Would you like to be an elf? _____ Why or why not? _____

Page 75

Elves and Fairies

Find the word for each clue. Each word is made from the letters in these 3 words:

ELVES AND FAIRIES

good with burgers **fries**
shirts have two **sleeves**
opposite of more **less**
forest animal with hooves **deer**
not dead **alive**
sun does this early **rises**
water goes down this **drain**
land with water around it **island**
not a captive **free**

Draw an elf. Then write what you think the elf might say.

Fairies are thought to have magic. What are 4 magical things that fairies might be able to do?

1. _____
2. _____
3. _____
4. _____

Fairy and ferry are homophones. Write a homophone for each word below.
flower **flour**   sun **son**   merry **Mary/marry**
wood **would**   root **route**   reed **read**

Page 76

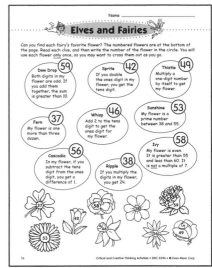

Elves and Fairies

Can you find each fairy's favorite flower? The numbered flowers are at the bottom of the page. Read each clue, and then write the number of the flower in the circle. You will use each flower only once, so you may want to cross them out as you go.

Dew Drop **59** Both digits in my flower are odd. If you add them together, the sum is greater than 10.

Sprite **42** If you double the ones digit in my flower, you get the tens digit.

Thistle **49** Multiply a one-digit number by itself to get my flower.

Fern **37** My flower is one more than three dozen.

Whisp **46** Add 2 to the tens digit to get the ones digit for my flower.

Sunshine **53** My flower is a prime number between 38 and 55.

Cascadia **56** In my flower, if you subtract the tens digit from the ones digit, you get a difference of 1.

Ripple **38** If you multiply the digits in my flower, you get 24.

Ivy **58** My flower is even. It is greater than 55 and less than 60. It is not a multiple of 7.

Page 77

Dragons

What if dragons were real? Write 3 things that people might do.

1. _____
2. _____
3. _____

Use the clues to find the name of each dragon. Write each name near its description.
• Flame is smaller than Talon.
• Scalia lost all of her teeth when she tried to eat cement.
• Talon is bigger than Scalia.

Scalia has spots.
Talon is the biggest.
Flame has the sharpest teeth.

It takes 57 weeks for dragons to hatch from their eggs. How many days is that?
399 days

Adult dragons have 226 teeth. How many teeth do 9 dragons have?
2,034 teeth

Your job is to take some of the dragon's treasure. You do not have any weapons. The dragon never leaves her cave without a reason. What is your plan?
_____

Page 78

Dragons

How are an alligator and a dragon the same? How are they different? Write 3 ways for each.

Same	Different

Describe what you think a dragon smells like. Use your imagination and be descriptive!
_____

ANALOGIES
scales : dragon :: feathers : **bird**
dragon : fly :: fish : **swim**
cave : dragon :: hive : **bee**

Doug the Dragon is fond of knights. He ate 18 of them in 3 days! He ate half as many on the first day as he did on the second day. On the third day, he gorged himself by eating the same number of knights that he'd eaten in the first 2 days. How many knights did Doug eat on each day?
Day 1: **3**   Day 2: **6**   Day 3: **9**

Page 79

Dragons

You found a rather large egg in your backyard. A few weeks later, the egg hatched. You are now the owner of a baby dragon. Of course, you decide to keep it. Answer the questions about how you will manage to raise your new pet.

What will you name your dragon? _____

What will you feed it? _____

What are 3 challenges that you will have to face while raising your dragon?
1. _____
2. _____
3. _____

Draw your dragon.

What will you train your dragon to do?
_____

What will you do with your dragon when it is full-grown?
_____

Page 80

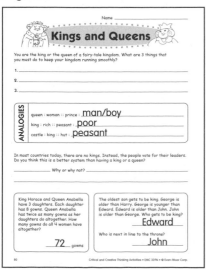

Kings and Queens

You are the king or the queen of a fairy-tale kingdom. What are 3 things that you must do to keep your kingdom running smoothly?

1. _____
2. _____
3. _____

ANALOGIES
queen : woman :: prince : **man/boy**
king : rich :: peasant : **poor**
castle : king :: hut : **peasant**

In most countries today, there are no kings. Instead, the people vote for their leaders. Do you think this is a better system than having a king or a queen?
_____ Why or why not? _____

King Horace and Queen Anabella have 3 daughters. Each daughter has 8 gowns. Queen Anabella has twice as many gowns as her daughters do altogether. How many gowns do all 4 women have altogether?
72 gowns

The oldest son gets to be king. George is older than Harry. George is younger than Edward. Edward is older than John. John is older than George. Who gets to be king?
Edward
Who is next in line to the throne?
John

Page 81

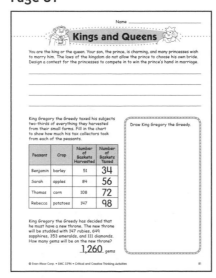

Kings and Queens

You are the king or the queen. Your son, the prince, is charming, and many princesses wish to marry him. The laws of the kingdom do not allow the prince to choose his own bride. Design a contest for the princesses to compete in to win the prince's hand in marriage.

King Gregory the Greedy taxed his subjects two-thirds of everything they harvested from their small farms. Fill in the chart to show how much his tax collectors took from each of the peasants.

Peasant	Crop	Number of Baskets Harvested	Number of Baskets Taxed
Benjamin	barley	51	**34**
Sarah	apples	84	**56**
Thomas	corn	108	**72**
Rebecca	potatoes	147	**98**

Draw King Gregory the Greedy.

King Gregory the Greedy has decided that he must have a new throne. The new throne will be studded with 147 rubies, 649 sapphires, 353 emeralds, and 111 diamonds. How many gems will be on the new throne?
1,260 gems

Page 82

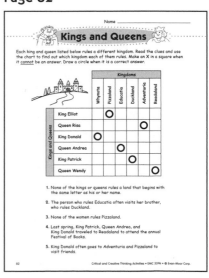

Kings and Queens

Each king and queen listed below rules a different kingdom. Read the clues and use the chart to find out which kingdom each of them rules. Make an X in a square when it cannot be an answer. Draw a circle when it is a correct answer.

		Kingdoms				
		Whyneta	Pizzaland	Educatia	Duckland	Adventuria	Readaland
	King Elliot		O				
	Queen Risa					O	
	King Donald	O					
	Queen Andrea			O			
	King Patrick				O		
	Queen Wendy						O

1. None of the kings or queens rules a land that begins with the same letter as his or her name.
2. The person who rules Educatia often visits her brother, who rules Duckland.
3. None of the women rules Pizzaland.
4. Last spring, King Patrick, Queen Andrea, and King Donald traveled to Readaland to attend the annual Festival of Books.
5. King Donald often goes to Adventuria and Pizzaland to visit friends.

© Evan-Moor Corp. • EMC 3394 • Critical and Creative Thinking Activities

Page 83

Magic

Many authors have created mythical places where magic is possible. Some examples include Narnia, Oz, and Hogwarts. If you could visit a magical world, which one would you choose?

_____ Why? _____

Number the magical abilities from 1 to 8 according to how much you would like to have them. The one you would like the most should be number 1.

___ fly
___ turn people into stone
___ move people and things
___ turn invisible
___ speak to animals
___ predict the future
___ make food appear
___ turn straw into gold

Ana must give the evil witch 140 gold coins or the witch will turn Ana's husband into a frog. Luckily, Ana has a magic pot that makes 1 gold coin every 2 minutes. How long will it take to make all of the gold coins Ana needs?

__4__ hours __40__ minutes

Ana turned on the magic pot at 2:15. At what time will she have enough coins?

__6:55__

Write a sentence using the words *magic, wizard, want,* and *spaghetti.*

Page 84

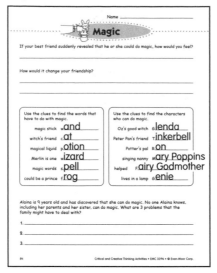

Magic

If your best friend suddenly revealed that he or she could do magic, how would you feel?

_____

How would it change your friendship?

_____

Use the clues to find the words that have to do with magic.

magic stick w__and__
witch's friend c__at__
magical liquid p__otion__
Merlin is one w__izard__
magic words s__pell__
could be a prince f__rog__

Use the clues to find the characters who can do magic.

Oz's good witch G__lenda__
Peter Pan's friend T__inkerbell__
Potter's pal R__on__
singing nanny M__ary Poppins__
helped F__airy Godmother__
lives in a lamp G__enie__

Alaina is 9 years old and has discovered that she can do magic. No one Alaina knows, including her parents and her sister, can do magic. What are 3 problems that the family might have to deal with?

1. _____
2. _____
3. _____

Page 85

Magic

Fill in the chart to tell what you would do with each magical item. Each item will work only one time.

Magical Item	What It Does	What You Will Use It For
key	will open any lock	
carpet	will take you anywhere in the world	
box	can be opened only by you	
book	will tell you anything you need to know	
pot	will make any food you want	
crystal ball	will allow you to see into the future	
cloak	will make you invisible	
potion I	will make someone tell the truth	
potion II	will make you super smart for one hour	
potion III	will turn you into any animal for one hour	

Page 86

Mythical Creatures

Fill in the missing vowels for the mythical creatures. Then find the words in the word search. If you don't know the creature, try finding it in the word search first.

tr__O__ll
c__E__nt__AU__r
dr__A__g__O__n
f__A____I__ry
b__A__s__I__l__I__sk
m__E__rm__A____I__d
__E__lf
ph__O__ __E__n__I__x
gn__O__m__E__
cycl__O__ps
w__E__r__E__w__O__lf
g__O__bl__I__n
__U__n__I__c__O__rn

```
B A S I L I S K Y K B G
P B A F L O W E R E W O
V C I M O L V M U D P B
Q Y X N R P Y E F N P L
E C E N T A U R O O U I
F L S H E E P M G N P N
A O F T D A E A Y I P H
I P H O E N I X S Y C
R S N O G A R D M G N
Y L I O N N R O C I N U
```

Word Search Challenge:
Find 3 animals that are *not* mythical.

__lion__ __sheep__ __puppy__

Finish the tongue twisters.

Two terrible trolls _____

Gorf the Goofy Goblin _____

Meera Mermaid made _____

Willy Werewolf was _____

Page 87

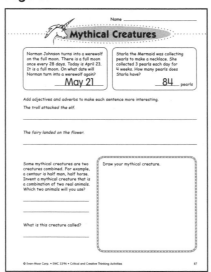

Mythical Creatures

Norman Johnson turns into a werewolf on the full moon. There is a full moon once every 28 days. Today is April 23. It is a full moon. On what date will Norman turn into a werewolf again?

__May 21__

Starla the Mermaid was collecting pearls to make a necklace. She collected 3 pearls each day for 4 weeks. How many pearls does Starla have?

__84__ pearls

Add adjectives and adverbs to make each sentence more interesting.
The troll attacked the elf.

_____

The fairy landed on the flower.

_____

Some mythical creatures are two creatures combined. For example, a centaur is half man, half horse. Invent a mythical creature that is a combination of two real animals. Which two animals will you use?

_____

What is this creature called?

_____

Draw your mythical creature.

Page 88

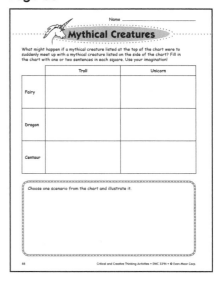

Mythical Creatures

What might happen if a mythical creature listed at the top of the chart were to suddenly meet up with a mythical creature listed on the side of the chart? Fill in the chart with one or two sentences in each square. Use your imagination!

	Troll	Unicorn
Fairy		
Dragon		
Centaur		

Choose one scenario from the chart and illustrate it.

Page 89

My Bike

The seat is one part of a bicycle. How many other parts can you name?

1. handlebars
2. wheel
3. tire
4. chain
5. spokes
6. gearshift
7. brakes
8. pedals

Trace a path showing how you can visit 12 friends on your way home. You may *not* visit any house more than once or retrace your own path.

Complete each sentence.

My bike _____

_____ my bike.

_____ my bike.

Page 90

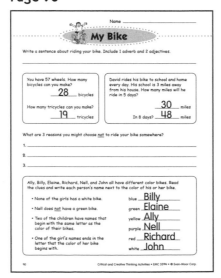

My Bike

Write a sentence about riding your bike. Include 1 adverb and 2 adjectives.

_____

You have 57 wheels. How many bicycles can you make?

__28__ bicycles

How many tricycles can you make?

__19__ tricycles

David rides his bike to school and home every day. His school is 3 miles away from his house. How many miles will he ride in 5 days?

__30__ miles

In 8 days? __48__ miles

What are 3 reasons you might choose *not* to ride your bike somewhere?

1. _____
2. _____
3. _____

Ally, Billy, Elaine, Richard, Nell, and John all have different color bikes. Read the clues and write each person's name next to the color of his or her bike.

• None of the girls has a white bike.
• Nell does *not* have a green bike.
• Two of the children have names that begin with the same letter as the color of their bikes.
• One of the girl's names ends in the letter that the color of her bike begins with.

blue __Billy__
green __Elaine__
yellow __Ally__
purple __Nell__
red __Richard__
white __John__

Page 91

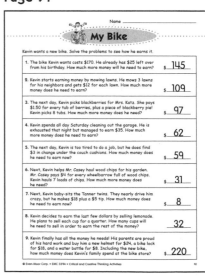

My Bike

Kevin wants a new bike. Solve the problems to see how he earns it.

1. The bike Kevin wants costs $170. He already has $25 left over from his birthday. How much more money will he need to earn? **$ 145**

2. Kevin starts earning money by mowing lawns. He mows 3 lawns for his neighbors and gets $12 for each lawn. How much more money does he need to earn? **$ 109**

3. The next day, Kevin picks blackberries for Mrs. Katz. She pays $1.50 for every tub of berries, plus a piece of blackberry pie! Kevin picks 8 tubs. How much more money does he need? **$ 97**

4. Kevin spends all day Saturday cleaning out the garage. He is exhausted that night but managed to earn $35. How much more money does he need to earn? **$ 62**

5. The next day, Kevin is too tired to do a job, but he does find $3 in change under the couch cushions. How much money does he need to earn now? **$ 59**

6. Next, Kevin helps Mr. Casey haul wood chips for his garden. Mr. Casey pays $4 for every wheelbarrow full of wood chips. Kevin hauls 7 loads of chips. How much more money does he need? **$ 31**

7. Next, Kevin baby-sits the Tanner twins. They nearly drive him crazy, but he makes $18 plus a $5 tip. How much money does he need to earn now? **$ 8**

8. Kevin decides to earn the last few dollars by selling lemonade. He plans to sell each cup at a quarter. How many cups will he need to sell in order to earn the rest of the money? **32**

9. Kevin finally has all the money he needs! His parents are proud of his hard work and buy him a new helmet for $24, a bike lock for $18, and a water bottle for $8. Including the new bike, how much money does Kevin's family spend at the bike store? **$ 220**

Page 92

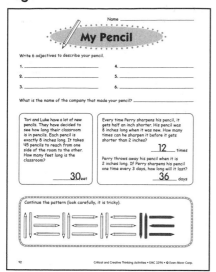

My Pencil

Write 6 adjectives to describe your pencil.

1. _____ 4. _____
2. _____ 5. _____
3. _____ 6. _____

What is the name of the company that made your pencil? _____

Tori and Luke have a lot of new pencils. They have decided to see how long their classroom is in pencils. Each pencil is exactly 8 inches long. It takes 45 pencils to reach from one side of the room to the other. How many feet long is the classroom?

30 feet

Every time Perry sharpens his pencil, it gets half an inch shorter. His pencil was 8 inches long when it was new. How many times can he sharpen it before it gets shorter than 2 inches?

12 times

Perry throws away his pencil when it is 2 inches long. If Perry sharpens his pencil one time every 3 days, how long will it last?

36 days

Continue the pattern (look carefully, it is tricky).

Page 93

My Pencil

Which do you like better—traditional wooden pencils or mechanical pencils?

_____ Why? _____

What materials were used to make your pencil? _____

Try to balance your pencil on your finger for 10 seconds. Could you do it?
☐ yes
☐ no

Draw a realistic picture of your pencil.

Besides writing and erasing, what are some other things that you can do with a pencil?

1. _____
2. _____
3. _____
4. _____
5. _____
6. _____

How many pencils are in your desk right now?

Guess: _____ Actual number: _____

Page 94

My Pencil

What would these everyday objects say if they could talk?

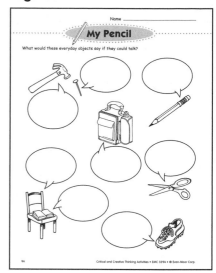

Page 95

My Hands

Write 4 adjectives to describe your hands.

1. _____ 3. _____
2. _____

How many fingers (not including thumbs) are in your classroom right now?

_____ fingers

Grandma has decided to knit mittens for all of her grandchildren. She has 9 grandchildren. It takes 3 hours to make one mitten. How many hours of knitting will it take Grandma to make all of the mittens?

54 hours

What are 3 things that would be much harder to do if you did not have thumbs?

1. _____
2. _____
3. _____

What do they say?

HAhandND	hand hand hand hand hand hand DECK	HAND ME / HAND ME / HAND ME
hand in hand	all hands on deck	hand-me-downs

Page 96

My Hands

What does each expression mean?

"It's out of my hands." Someone else is taking care of it.

"I did it with my bare hands." I did it without tools or by myself.

"She has the upper hand." She has the advantage.

"A bird in the hand is worth two in the bush." What you possess is more valuable than something you don't have.

ANALOGIES

hand : wrist :: foot : ankle
fingers : ten :: ears : two
glove : hand :: sock : foot
boy : hand :: kitten : paw

Why do you think we have fingernails? _____

Why do you think most people can't bend their fingers backward? _____

Do you think it is okay to tell a lie if you cross your fingers behind your back? _____
Why or why not? _____

What is the sound of one hand clapping? _____

Page 97

My Hands

What kinds of fingerprints do you have? Follow the instructions to find out!
• Use a pencil to fill in the square on the right. Press hard and make it dark. You may need to go over it again as you make more prints.
• Press one of your fingertips on the square.
• Stick a piece of clear tape onto your fingertip.
• Place the tape in the box for that finger to see your print!

	Thumb	Index	Middle	Ring	Pinkie
RIGHT HAND					
	Thumb	Index	Middle	Ring	Pinkie
LEFT HAND					

Look at the different kinds of fingerprints below to help you identify yours. Label each of your prints with the appropriate number.

Loop | Double Loop | Central Pocket Loop | Plain Arch | Tented Arch | Plain Whorl | Accidental

Which kind of fingerprint do you have the most of? _____

Page 98

The Dictionary

What are 3 things that you can use a dictionary for?

1. _____
2. _____
3. _____

Write a definition that you might find in a dictionary for the word *dictionary*.

Richard has decided to read the entire dictionary. His plan is to read one page each day. There are 1,825 pages in Richard's dictionary. Make an X on the number line to show about how many years it will take Richard to read the entire book.

0 1 2 3 4 5 6 7 8

Ian has a different plan. He has decided to read 3 words in the dictionary each day. If both boys start on the same day, how many words will Ian have read when Richard is done?

5,475 words

If your name were in the dictionary, what word would be directly above it? What word would be directly below it?

_____ and _____

A large dictionary has about 500,000 words and definitions. How many do you think you know? _____

How many do you think your teacher knows? _____

Page 99

The Dictionary

Make as many smaller words as you can from the letters in this word:

DICTIONARY

1. _____ 6. _____ 11. _____
2. _____ 7. _____ 12. _____
3. _____ 8. _____ 13. _____
4. _____ 9. _____ 14. _____
5. _____ 10. _____ 15. _____

Would you rather use a dictionary in book form or a dictionary on the Internet?

_____ Why? _____

You do not know how to spell a word and need to look it up in the dictionary. Number the steps that you must take from 1 to 6.

4 Scan the page for your word.
1 Get the dictionary.
5 Find your word.
6 Write down the word correctly.
3 Use the guide words to find the correct page.
2 Open the dictionary to the letter your word begins with.

Jessica made a stack of dictionaries in her classroom. She used 28 dictionaries. The stack was 7 feet high. How many inches thick was each dictionary?

3 inches

Page 100

The Dictionary

In a dictionary, the guide words at the top of a page are the same as the first and last words on that page. For each pair of guide words below, write 3 other words that would appear on that page of the dictionary.

Guide Words	3 Words That Would Appear on the Page
car, comb	_____
vanilla, voice	_____
mindless, more	_____
tape, tiger	_____
nobody, nothing	_____
wild, write	_____
brand, bright	_____
arid, attract	_____

Page 101

Locks and Keys

Name _____

What are 10 things that you might need to open with a key?

1. _____ 6. _____
2. _____ 7. _____
3. _____ 8. _____
4. _____ 9. _____
5. _____ 10. _____

Use the clues to find the words. Each word rhymes with either *LOCK* or *KEY*.

has a trunk	tree
stone	rock
to speak	talk
look	see
on your leg	knee
on your foot	sock
hot drink	tea
tells the time	clock
group of sheep	flock
not a prisoner	free

Shelby has a combination lock for her bike. Use the clues to find her combination.

• The combination is a 3-digit number.
• The first and third digits are even.
• The middle digit is 3 more than the last digit.
• The middle digit is 7 more than the first digit.
• If you add all of the digits together, you get 17.

What is Shelby's combination?

296

© Evan-Moor Corp. • EMC 3394 • Critical and Creative Thinking Activities   101

Page 102

Locks and Keys

Name _____

Do you think it is a good idea to have a secret house key hidden somewhere near your house?

Why or why not? _____

Why do you think keys are usually made from metal instead of plastic or wood?

_____

What do these say?

house key

lock up before you go

keyhole

What are 3 reasons a person might decide *not* to lock the door when he or she leaves the house?

1. _____
2. _____
3. _____

Write a sentence using the words *lock, key, secret,* and *watermelon.*

102   Critical and Creative Thinking Activities • EMC 3394 • © Evan-Moor Corp.

Page 103

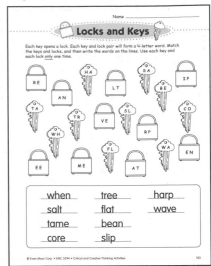

Locks and Keys

Name _____

Each key opens a lock. Each key and lock pair will form a 4-letter word. Match the keys and locks, and then write the words on the lines. Use each key and each lock only one time.

when	tree	harp
salt	flat	wave
tame	bean	
core	slip	

© Evan-Moor Corp. • EMC 3394 • Critical and Creative Thinking Activities   103

Page 104

Thank you.   **Manners**   You're welcome.

Name _____

Do you think that manners are important? _____

Why or why not? _____

Do you think that it is possible to be too polite? _____

Why or why not? _____

Find the word for each clue. Each word is made from the letters in this word:

PLEASE

friend	pal
ocean	sea
long, skinny fish	eel
liquid in a tree	sap
aquatic mammal	seal
do this to an orange	peel
half price	sale
do at night	sleep
light-colored	pale

Aunt Clara is more polite than Aunt Edna. Aunt Edna is less polite than Aunt Martha. Aunt Petunia is just plain rude.

Write T if the statement is true, F if it is false, and C if you can't tell.

T Aunt Martha is more polite than Aunt Edna.

C Aunt Clara is the most polite aunt.

T Aunt Martha might be more polite than Aunt Clara.

T Aunt Petunia is less polite than Aunt Edna.

C Aunt Petunia never says "please."

104   Critical and Creative Thinking Activities • EMC 3394 • © Evan-Moor Corp.

Page 105

Thank you.   **Manners**   You're welcome.

Name _____

Do you have better table manners at home or at a friend's house? _____

Why? _____

Carrie is having dinner with a new friend and her family. She does *not* like the food. What should Carrie do?

Number the table manners from 1 to 7. The one you think is most important should be number 1.

___ saying "please" and "thank you"
___ not slurping soup
___ not reaching for things
___ chewing with your mouth closed
___ keeping elbows off the table
___ using silverware correctly
___ using a quiet voice

Would you rather have a friend who always interrupted you when you were talking or one who always chewed with his or her mouth open?

Why? _____

Brent usually has excellent table manners, but tonight, his manners are terrible. List 3 possible reasons.

1. _____
2. _____
3. _____

© Evan-Moor Corp. • EMC 3394 • Critical and Creative Thinking Activities   105

Page 106

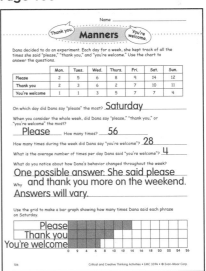

Thank you.   **Manners**   You're welcome.

Name _____

Dana decided to do an experiment. Each day for a week, she kept track of all the times she said "please," "thank you," and "you're welcome." Use the chart to answer the questions.

	Mon.	Tues.	Wed.	Thurs.	Fri.	Sat.	Sun.
Please	2	5	6	8	9	14	12
Thank you	2	3	6	2	7	10	11
You're welcome	1	1	3	5	7	7	4

On which day did Dana say "please" the most? **Saturday**

When you consider the whole week, did Dana say "please," "thank you," or "you're welcome" the most?

Please   How many times? **56**

How many times during the week did Dana say "you're welcome"? **28**

What is the average number of times per day Dana said "you're welcome"? **4**

What do you notice about how Dana's behavior changed throughout the week?

Why **One possible answer: She said please and thank you more on the weekend. Answers will vary.**

Use the grid to make a bar graph showing how many times Dana said each phrase on Saturday.

Please	
Thank you	
You're welcome	
	0 2 4 6 8 10 12 14 16 18 20 22 24 26

106   Critical and Creative Thinking Activities • EMC 3394 • © Evan-Moor Corp.

Page 107

Hats and Caps

Name _____

What is the main difference between a hat and a cap?

_____

What are 5 different reasons a person might wear a hat?

1. _____
2. _____
3. _____
4. _____
5. _____

Jeremy wears his baseball cap every Friday. Taylor wears his baseball cap every other day. Today is Friday, April 3. Both boys are wearing their caps. How many days will it be until both boys are wearing their caps on the same day again?

14 days

What date will it be? **April 17**

Mike the Magician can pull rabbits out of his hat. Yesterday, he pulled out three times as many rabbits as he did today. He pulled 68 rabbits out of his hat altogether. How many did he pull out on each day?

Yesterday: **51**

Today: **17**

Skyler wants to ride his bike, but he cannot find his bike helmet. What should he do?

© Evan-Moor Corp. • EMC 3394 • Critical and Creative Thinking Activities   107

Page 108

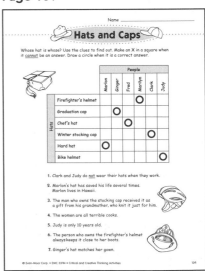

Hats and Caps

Name _____

What are 4 different reasons a person might wear a helmet?

1. _____
2. _____
3. _____
4. _____

Use the clues to find the words. Each word rhymes with either *HAT* or *CAP.*

furry pet	cat
to sleep in the day	nap
to touch lightly	tap
conversation	chat
noise with hands	clap
for baseball	bat
spoiled child	brat
navigation tool	map
open-handed hit	slap

Cody wears a different color baseball cap to school each day. The colors are green, yellow, blue, orange, and red. He wears primary colors on the first 3 days of the week. He does *not* wear a green cap on Friday. He does *not* wear a red cap on Monday or Tuesday. He does *not* wear a yellow cap on Tuesday. Write the colors of the caps.

Monday: **yellow**
Tuesday: **blue**
Wednesday: **red**
Thursday: **green**
Friday: **orange**

ANALOGIES

hard hat : construction worker :: stocking hat : **skier/skater**

firefighter's helmet : red :: chef's hat : **white**

head : hat :: waist : **belt**

108   Critical and Creative Thinking Activities • EMC 3394 • © Evan-Moor Corp.

Page 109

Hats and Caps

Name _____

Whose hat is whose? Use the clues to find out. Make an X in a square when it *cannot* be an answer. Draw a circle when it is a correct answer.

		People				
		Marlon	Ginger	Fred	Marilyn	Clark	Judy
Hats	Firefighter's helmet				○		
	Graduation cap		○				
	Chef's hat			○			
	Winter stocking cap					○	
	Hard hat	○					
	Bike helmet						○

1. Clark and Judy do *not* wear their hats when they work.
2. Marlon's hat has saved his life several times. Marlon lives in Hawaii.
3. The man who owns the stocking cap received it as a gift from his grandmother, who knit it just for him.
4. The women are all terrible cooks.
5. Judy is only 10 years old.
6. The person who owns the firefighter's helmet always keeps it close to her boots.
7. Ginger's hat matches her gown.

© Evan-Moor Corp. • EMC 3394 • Critical and Creative Thinking Activities   109

Critical and Creative Thinking Activities • EMC 3394 • © Evan-Moor Corp.

Presents

Pretend that you can give any present you want to each of the people below. What will you give?

your best friend ___
your mom ___
your teacher ___
a blind child ___
a child in the hospital ___
the president ___

Laura got 16 presents for her birthday. Half of them were games. Three-fourths of the games were board games. How many board games did Laura get?

6 board games

6 children got presents. Read the clues, and then write each child's name next to his or her present.

- Ethan's present does not have a bow.
- Josie's present is not the smallest.
- Mandy's present has dots. So does Aiden's.
- Kathy's and Josie's presents both have bows.
- Carlos's and Mandy's presents are both in gift bags.

Aiden · Kathy · Mandy · Ethan · Josie · Carlos

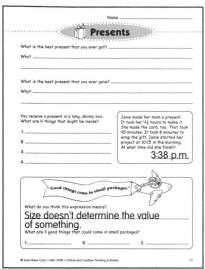

Presents

What is the best present that you ever got? ___
Why? ___

What is the best present that you ever gave? ___
Why? ___

You receive a present in a long, skinny box. What are 4 things that might be inside?
1. ___
2. ___
3. ___
4. ___

Janie made her mom a present. It took her 4½ hours to make it. She made the card, too. That took 45 minutes. It took 8 minutes to wrap the gift. Janie started her project at 10:15 in the morning. At what time did she finish?

3:38 p.m.

"Good things come in small packages."

What do you think this expression means?
Size doesn't determine the value of something.

What are 3 good things that could come in small packages?
1. ___ 2. ___ 3. ___

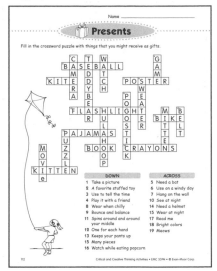

Presents

Fill in the crossword puzzle with things that you might receive as gifts.

C T W G A M
BASEBALL M D T C M
K I T E D C H POSTER A
R Y T W E
A O O A
FLASHLIGHT S T E M B
R U L I I
PAJAMAS E L K K
U I E
PUZZLE BOOK CRAYONS
M Z O T
O L K
K I T T E N
e

DOWN
1 Take a picture
2 A favorite stuffed toy
3 Use to tell the time
4 Play it with a friend
8 Wear when chilly
9 Bounce and balance
11 Spins around and around your middle
12 One for each hand
13 Keeps your pants up
15 Many pieces
16 Watch while eating popcorn

ACROSS
5 Need a bat
6 Use on a windy day
7 Hang on the wall
10 See at night
14 Need a helmet
15 Wear at night
17 Read me
18 Bright colors
19 Meows

Chores

Do you think that children should have chores to do each day? ___
Why or why not? ___

Should children be paid for doing chores? ___
Why or why not? ___

The list of chores below has gotten all mixed up! Rewrite it so that each verb goes with the correct noun.

Chores

dust the dog → **dust the furniture**
dry the garden → **dry the dishes**
fold the windows → **fold the laundry**
get the counters → **get the mail**
weed the floor → **weed the garden**
feed the laundry → **feed the dog**
wash the mail → **wash the windows**
make the furniture → **make the bed**
wipe the bed → **wipe the counters**
sweep the dishes → **sweep the floor**

Mark lives on a farm. Every morning, he spends 28 minutes milking the cow. Then he spends 17 minutes feeding the chickens and collecting the eggs. It takes him 54 minutes to feed the horses and shovel out the stalls. How long does it take Mark to do his chores?

99 minutes

If Mark starts at 6:30 in the morning, at what time will he be done?

8:09

Chores

What is a good chore for...
a 3-year-old? ___
a 5-year-old? ___
an 8-year-old? ___
a 10-year-old? ___

John, Jake, and Jim must weed the garden. There are 15 rows to weed. It takes half an hour to weed 1 row. How long will it take the three boys to weed the whole garden?

2½ hours

ANALOGIES

towel : dishes :: mop : **floor**
sweep : broom :: weed : **hoe/hands**
chore : home :: test : **school**

Christine is very good about doing her chores every day. Yesterday, she did not do any of her chores. List 3 possible reasons.
1. ___
2. ___
3. ___

"Many hands make light work."

What do you think this expression means? **The job is easier when people work together.**

Chores

The Johnsons use a chore chart to show which chores each of their 4 children will do each week. Read the rules, and then fill in the chart with the children's names.

Kelsey · Tom · Amelia · Maya

	Monday	Tuesday	Wednesday	Thursday	Friday
Empty the dishwasher	Tom	Amelia	Maya	Kelsey	Maya
Set the table	Tom	Maya	Amelia	Kelsey	Tom
Help with dinner	Tom	Kelsey	Tom	Amelia	Maya
Fold laundry	Amelia	Kelsey	Tom	Maya	Tom
Feed the cats	Maya	Kelsey	Tom	Kelsey	Amelia
Sweep the floors	Kelsey	Tom	Kelsey	Tom	Kelsey
Take out the garbage	Kelsey	Tom	Kelsey	Tom	Kelsey
Tidy the living room	Kelsey	Tom	Kelsey	Tom	Kelsey

Answers will vary but rules must be followed. One possible solution is shown.

2. Amelia and Maya each do a different chore each day, but they do not take out the garbage, sweep the floors, or tidy the living room.
3. Both Kelsey and Tom must do each chore at least one time a week.
4. No child may do the same chore two days in a row.

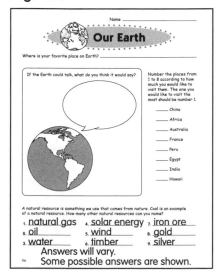

Our Earth

Where is your favorite place on Earth? ___

If the Earth could talk, what do you think it would say?

Number the places from 1 to 8 according to how much you would like to visit them. The one you would like to visit the most should be number 1.

___ China
___ Africa
___ Australia
___ France
___ Peru
___ Egypt
___ India
___ Hawaii

A natural resource is something we use that comes from nature. Coal is an example of a natural resource. How many other natural resources can you name?

1. **natural gas** 4. **solar energy** 7. **iron ore**
2. **oil** 5. **wind** 8. **gold**
3. **water** 6. **timber** 9. **silver**

Answers will vary. Some possible answers are shown.

Our Earth

How does recycling help the Earth? ___
How does driving less help the Earth? ___
How does using less electricity help the Earth? ___

If you could fly around the Earth in an airplane, you would have to fly 24,900 miles. An airplane flies about 500 miles an hour. About how many hours would it take you to circle the Earth?

50 hours

Where in the world are you?
Continent: ___
Country: ___
State: ___
County: ___
City: ___
Street: ___

Add 2 more each time, and then tell what they are.

Atlantic, Indian, **Pacific, Southern Arctic—oceans**
Australia, **Africa, South America, etc.—continents**
Sahara, Death Valley, **Mojave, Gobi—deserts**
France, Spain, **Germany, Italy—European countries**
Cuba, Hawaii, New Zealand, **Iceland, Japan—islands**

Our Earth

Use the initials and the clues to help you name the landmarks and places.

in New York S**tatue** of L**iberty**
in Paris E**iffel** T**ower**
in Egypt G**reat** P**yramids**
piranhas live here A**mazon** R**iver**
tallest mountain M**ount** E**verest**
smallest continent A**ustralia**
very big hole G**rand** C**anyon**
where movie stars live H**ollywood**
cold continent A**ntarctica**
European country that is shaped like a boot I**taly**
home of Old Faithful Y**ellowstone National Park**
where Mickey Mouse lives D**isneyland**
United States' neighbor to the north C**anada**
where the president of the USA lives the W**hite** H**ouse**
largest of the Great Lakes L**ake** S**uperior**
largest state in the U.S. A**laska**
big, beautiful white building in India T**aj** M**ahal**
volcano in northwest USA M**ount** S**aint** H**elens**
big barrier in Asia G**reat** W**all** of C**hina**
big body of water P**acific** O**cean**

Page 119

Garbage

Name _____

Write a sentence that is always true about garbage.

Write a sentence that is sometimes true about garbage.

Write a sentence that is never true about garbage.

Find the word for each clue. Each word is made from the letters in this word:

GARBAGE

use to carry things	**bag**
to snatch	**grab**
large, furry animal	**bear**
how old you are	**age**
to boast	**brag**
flat boat	**barge**

Each person in the United States produces about 1,609 pounds of garbage a year! About how many pounds of garbage did your family produce last year?

_____ pounds

About how many pounds of garbage have you produced in your life so far?

_____ pounds

What are 3 ways that your family could produce less garbage?

1. _____
2. _____
3. _____

© Evan-Moor Corp. • EMC 3394 • Critical and Creative Thinking Activities   119

Page 120

Garbage

Name _____

When we reuse things instead of throwing them away, we save resources and we don't fill up landfills. How could you reuse each of these items?

soda bottle _____

egg carton _____

old magazines _____

torn shirt _____

old CDs and DVDs _____

SYNONYMS

Garbage is a synonym for trash. Write a synonym for each word below.

bin **container/receptacle**
smelly **stinky**
slimy **gooey**
broken **ruined/shattered**
soiled **dirty**
disgusting **gross/revolting**

Mr. Smith takes out his garbage on Mondays and Thursdays. Mr. Jones takes out his garbage once every 3 days. Both men have taken out their garbage today. Today is Thursday, March 6. On what date will both men take out their garbage on the same day again?

Monday, March 24

What are 3 bad things that would happen if no one ever took out the garbage?

1. _____
2. _____
3. _____

120   Critical and Creative Thinking Activities • EMC 3394 • © Evan-Moor Corp.

Page 121

Garbage

Name _____

Some archaeologists study the garbage of ancient cultures to learn about how people lived. What can you learn about the Smith family by studying their garbage? Write it about below.

Found in Smith Family's Garbage and Recycling
- rice cakes bag
- diet soda bottle
- wilted lettuce leaves
- carrot peelings
- tomato stems
- broken mousetrap
- chocolate cake mix box
- frosting container
- 10 half-burned candles
- crumpled wrapping paper
- ice-cream carton
- school lunch calendar
- town pool schedule
- sugarless gum wrappers
- dead flowers
- *American Girl* magazine
- *Boys' Life* magazine
- 3 dog food cans
- large pizza box
- lice shampoo bottle
- tofu container
- nonfat yogurt container
- allergy pill bottle
- microwave popcorn bag
- broken Beatles CD
- veggie burger box
- hamburger bun bag
- onion skins
- 2 lottery tickets
- unidentifiable moldy stuff

What are 5 things that you know about this family?
1. _____
2. _____
3. _____
4. _____
5. _____

What are 5 things that are probably true about this family?
1. _____
2. _____
3. _____
4. _____
5. _____

What are 5 things that might be true about this family?
1. _____
2. _____
3. _____
4. _____
5. _____

© Evan-Moor Corp. • EMC 3394 • Critical and Creative Thinking Activities   121

Page 122

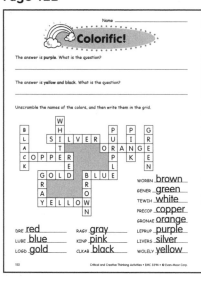

Colorific!

Name _____

The answer is purple. What is the question?

_____

The answer is yellow and black. What is the question?

_____

Unscramble the names of the colors, and then write them in the grid.

[crossword grid with: WHITE, SILVER, PURPLE, PINK, GREEN, BLACK, ORANGE, COPPER, GOLD, BLUE, GRAY, YELLOW, BROWN]

WORBN	**brown**
GENER	**green**
TEWIH	**white**
PRECOP	**copper**
GRONAE	**orange**
DRE	**red**
LUBE	**blue**
LOGD	**gold**
RAGY	**gray**
KINP	**pink**
LEPRUP	**purple**
LIVERS	**silver**
WOLELY	**yellow**
CLKAB	**black**

122   Critical and Creative Thinking Activities • EMC 3394 • © Evan-Moor Corp.

Page 123

Colorific!

Name _____

Why do you think many fire engines and all stop signs are red?

_____

Why do you think people who work in a hospital often wear white?

_____

Anna has 3 shirts: yellow, orange, and red. She has 3 pairs of pants: blue, purple, and green. How many different combinations of shirts and pants can Anna make?

9 combinations

If you put 6 blue marbles, 6 yellow marbles, and 6 red marbles in a bag, what are the chances of getting a blue marble the first time you choose one?

1 in 3

How many times would you have to draw from the bag to be sure you chose a blue marble?

13

What are 3 problems that you would have if you could see only in black and white?

1. _____
2. _____
3. _____

ANALOGIES

yellow : school bus :: green : **grass/"Go" light/Kermit**
primary : blue :: secondary : **green/orange/purple**
red : embarrassed :: green : **envious/jealous**

© Evan-Moor Corp. • EMC 3394 • Critical and Creative Thinking Activities   123

Page 124

Colorific!

Name _____

Here is a fun trick to play on your brain. Use red, blue, yellow, green, orange, purple, and brown to neatly color each of these color names. But do not color them with the correct colors. For example, do not color the word red with red. When you are done, try to say the colors of the words as fast as you can. Do not read the words, just say the colors. Can you do it?

RED YELLOW PURPLE GREEN ORANGE BLUE BROWN PURPLE ORANGE GREEN

Why do you think it is so hard to say the color names?

_____

124   Critical and Creative Thinking Activities • EMC 3394 • © Evan-Moor Corp.

Page 125

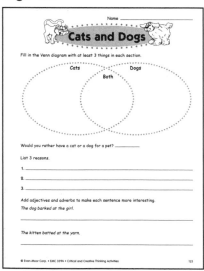

Cats and Dogs

Name _____

Fill in the Venn diagram with at least 3 things in each section.

Cats   Dogs
Both

Would you rather have a cat or a dog for a pet? _____

List 3 reasons.

1. _____
2. _____
3. _____

Add adjectives and adverbs to make each sentence more interesting.

The dog barked at the girl.

_____

The kitten batted at the yarn.

_____

© Evan-Moor Corp. • EMC 3394 • Critical and Creative Thinking Activities   125

Page 126

Cats and Dogs

Name _____

What do you think these expressions mean?

"Curiosity killed the cat."

Being too curious can get you into trouble.

"You can't teach an old dog new tricks."

It's harder to learn new things as you age.

Fluffy the Cat had 6 kittens. Each of her kittens had 6 kittens. Each of those kittens had 6 kittens. How many cats are there altogether?

217 cats

Marty's dog eats ⅔ pound of dog food every day. Marty has bought a 25-pound bag of dog food. How many days will it last?

37 days

Will there be any left over?

yes

How many different dog breeds can you name?

1. _____   5. _____   9. _____
2. _____   6. _____   10. _____
3. _____   7. _____   11. _____
4. _____   8. _____   12. _____

Why do you think most dogs can be trained to come, sit, stay, and even do tricks, while most cats cannot be easily trained to do those things?

_____

126   Critical and Creative Thinking Activities • EMC 3394 • © Evan-Moor Corp.

Page 127

Cats and Dogs

Name _____

Pretend that you get to adopt a kitten or a puppy. Answer the questions about how you will care for your new pet.

Will you get a kitten or a puppy? _____ Male or female? _____

What will you name him or her? _____

What supplies will you need to take care of your new pet?

_____
_____

What are 3 challenges that you may have with your new pet? How will you deal with these challenges?

1. Challenge: _____
   Solution: _____

2. Challenge: _____
   Solution: _____

3. Challenge: _____
   Solution: _____

What are 2 things that you look forward to doing with your new pet?

1. _____
2. _____

Draw your new pet.

© Evan-Moor Corp. • EMC 3394 • Critical and Creative Thinking Activities   127

Page 128

Name _____

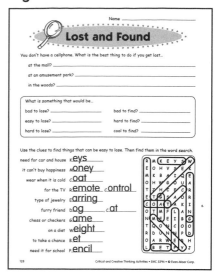

Lost and Found

You don't have a cellphone. What is the best thing to do if you get lost...

at the mall? _____

at an amusement park? _____

in the woods? _____

What is something that would be...

bad to lose? _____ bad to find? _____

easy to lose? _____ hard to find? _____

hard to lose? _____ cool to find? _____

Use the clues to find things that can be easy to lose. Then find them in the word search.

need for car and house	**keys**
it can't buy happiness	**money**
wear when it is cold	**coat**
for the TV	**remote control**
type of jewelry	**earring**
furry friend	**dog**, **cat**
chess or checkers	**game**
on a diet	**weight**
to take a chance	**bet**
need it for school	**pencil**

Critical and Creative Thinking Activities • EMC 3394 • © Evan-Moor Corp.

Page 129

Name _____

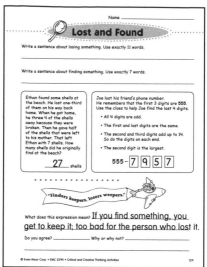

Lost and Found

Write a sentence about losing something. Use exactly 11 words.

_____

Write a sentence about finding something. Use exactly 7 words.

_____

Ethan found some shells at the beach. He lost one-third of them on his way back home. When he got home, he threw 4 of the shells away because they were broken. Then he gave half of the shells that were left to his mother. That left Ethan with 7 shells. How many shells did he originally find at the beach?

27 shells

Joe lost his friend's phone number. He remembers that the first 3 digits are **555**. Use the clues to help Joe find the last 4 digits.
• All 4 digits are odd.
• The first and last digits are the same.
• The second and third digits add up to 14. So do the digits on each end.
• The second digit is the largest.

555-**7957**

"Finders keepers, losers weepers."

What does this expression mean? **If you find something, you get to keep it; too bad for the person who lost it.**

Do you agree? ___ Why or why not? ___

© Evan-Moor Corp. • EMC 3394 • Critical and Creative Thinking Activities

---

Page 130

Name _____

Lost and Found

Pretend that you are going on a scavenger hunt in your classroom. Answer each question below to see if you can find the item on the information.

1. What is something in your classroom with exactly 3 colors? ___
2. How many legs (people, tables, chairs, animals) are in your classroom? ___
3. What is something in your classroom that begins with S? ___
4. Who in your classroom can play the piano? ___
5. What is your teacher's middle name? ___
6. What letter is to the right of E on a keyboard? ___
7. What is the capital of Peru? ___
8. How many inches tall is your desk? ___
9. What is something soft in your classroom? ___
10. On what day of the week is your birthday this year? ___
11. Which letter is the 19th in the alphabet? ___
12. What in your classroom are there more than 100 of? ___
13. What is the last word in the dictionary? ___
14. Who in your classroom will have the next birthday? ___
15. How many lights are in your classroom? ___
16. What is being served for hot lunch today? ___
17. What company published your math book? ___
18. How many minutes are there until your next recess? ___

Critical and Creative Thinking Activities • EMC 3394 • © Evan-Moor Corp.

Page 131

Name _____

Up, Up, and Away!

How many things can you think of that fly, float, or hover?

1. ___ 5. ___ 9. ___
2. ___ 6. ___ 10. ___
3. ___ 7. ___ 11. ___
4. ___ 8. ___ 12. ___

Draw and color a hot-air balloon for the basket.
• The balloon is blue.
• There is a yellow smiley face in the center.
• There is a circle of 12 orange dots around the face.
• There are 2 green horizontal stripes, one above the smiley face and one below it.

ANALOGIES

airplane : fly :: boat : **sail/float**

airplane : fuel :: kite : **wind**

sparrow : bird :: Superman : **superhero**

bat : cave :: bee : **hive**

© Evan-Moor Corp. • EMC 3394 • Critical and Creative Thinking Activities

---

Page 132

Name _____

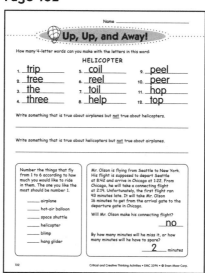

Up, Up, and Away!

How many 4-letter words can you make with the letters in this word:

HELICOPTER

1. **trip** 5. **coil** 9. **peel**
2. **tree** 6. **reel** 10. **peer**
3. **the** 7. **toil** 11. **hop**
4. **three** 8. **help** 12. **top**

Write something that is true about airplanes but not true about helicopters.

___

Write something that is true about helicopters but not true about airplanes.

___

Number the things that fly from 1 to 6 according to how much you would like to ride in them. The one you like the most should be number 1.
___ airplane
___ hot-air balloon
___ space shuttle
___ helicopter
___ blimp
___ hang glider

Mr. Olson is flying from Seattle to New York. His flight is supposed to depart Seattle at 8:42 and arrive in Chicago at 1:22. From Chicago, he will take a connecting flight at 2:19. Unfortunately, the first flight ran 43 minutes late. It will take Mr. Olson 16 minutes to get from the arrival gate to the departure gate in Chicago.

Will Mr. Olson make his connecting flight? **no**

By how many minutes will he miss it, or how many minutes will he have to spare? **2** minutes

© Evan-Moor Corp. • EMC 3394 • Critical and Creative Thinking Activities

---

Page 133

Name _____

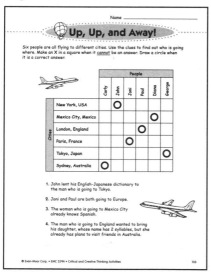

Up, Up, and Away!

Six people are all flying to different cities. Use the clues to find out who is going where. Make an X in a square when it cannot be an answer. Draw a circle when it is a correct answer.

		Carly	John	Joni	Paul	Diana	George
Cities	New York, USA		O				
	Mexico City, Mexico					O	
	London, England			O			
	Paris, France		O				
	Tokyo, Japan						O
	Sydney, Australia	O					

1. John lent his English-Japanese dictionary to the man who is going to Tokyo.
2. Joni and Paul are both going to Europe.
3. The woman who is going to Mexico City already knows Spanish.
4. The man who is going to England wanted to bring his daughter, whose name has 2 syllables, but she already has plans to visit friends in Australia.

© Evan-Moor Corp. • EMC 3394 • Critical and Creative Thinking Activities

---

Page 134

Name _____

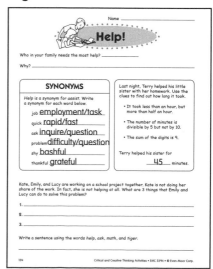

Help!

Who in your family needs the most help? ___

Why? ___

SYNONYMS

Help is a synonym for assist. Write a synonym for each word below.

job **employment/task**

quick **rapid/fast**

ask **inquire/question**

problem **difficulty/question**

shy **bashful**

thankful **grateful**

Last night, Terry helped his little sister with her homework. Use the clues to find out how long it took.
• It took less than an hour, but more than half an hour.
• The number of minutes is divisible by 5 but not by 10.
• The sum of the digits is 9.

Terry helped his sister for **45** minutes.

Kate, Emily, and Lucy are working on a school project together. Kate is not doing her share of the work. In fact, she is not helping at all. What are 3 things that Emily and Lucy can do to solve this problem?

1. ___
2. ___
3. ___

Write a sentence using the words help, ask, math, and tiger.

___

Critical and Creative Thinking Activities • EMC 3394 • © Evan-Moor Corp.

Page 135

Name _____

Help!

Jessica is having trouble with her math homework, but she won't ask anyone to help her. Give 3 possible reasons why she won't ask for help.

1. ___
2. ___
3. ___

Joanie helped her dad make cookies. They could fit 16 cookies on a cookie sheet (16 cookies = 1 batch). They had enough dough to make 200 cookies. How many batches did they make?

12½ batches

Jacob's mom helped him build a treehouse. For 3 weeks, they worked on the treehouse for 6 hours on Saturdays and for 2 hours after school on Mondays, Wednesdays, and Fridays. How many hours did Jacob work on the treehouse?

36 hours

Benny is 6 years old. Every day, he makes a big mess in his room. Every evening, when it is time to clean up, he begs his mom to help him. Should Benny's mom help him?

___ Why or why not? ___

Name something that you once needed help with but do not need help with now.

___

Name something that you need help with now but probably will not need help with when you are a little older.

___

© Evan-Moor Corp. • EMC 3394 • Critical and Creative Thinking Activities

---

Page 136

Name _____

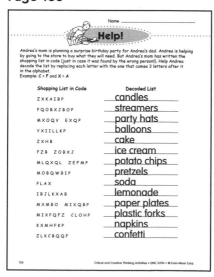

Help!

Andrea's mom is planning a surprise birthday party for Andrea's dad. Andrea is helping by going to the store to buy what they will need. But Andrea's mom has written the shopping list in code (just in case it was found by the wrong person). Help Andrea decode the list by replacing each letter with the one that comes 3 letters after it in the alphabet. Example: C = F and X = A

Shopping List in Code	Decoded List
Z X K A I B P	**candles**
P Q O B X J B O P	**streamers**
M X O Q V E X Q P	**party hats**
Y X I I L L K P	**balloons**
Z X H B	**cake**
F Z B Z O B X J	**ice cream**
M L Q X Q L Z E F M P	**potato chips**
M O B Q W B I P	**pretzels**
P I X	**soda**
I B J L K X A B	**lemonade**
M X M B O M I X Q B P	**paper plates**
M I X P Q F Z C L O H P	**plastic forks**
K X M H F K P	**napkins**
Z L K C B Q Q F	**confetti**

Critical and Creative Thinking Activities • EMC 3394 • © Evan-Moor Corp.

Page 137

Sticky Stuff

Name _____

What are 8 things that tape is used for?

1. _____   5. _____
2. _____   6. _____
3. _____   7. _____
4. _____   8. _____

Use the clues to find sticky things.

in a stick or a bottle	G**lue**
on a sandwich	P**eanut butter**
from the bees	H**oney**
comes on a roll	T**ape**
blow a bubble	G**um**
goes on pancakes	S**yrup**
from a tree	S**ap**
use to make cookies	D**ough**

You would not want to find honey on a computer keyboard. What are 7 other places where it would be very bad to find honey?

1. _____
2. _____
3. _____
4. _____
5. _____
6. _____
7. _____

Write a sentence using the words gum, bubble, stuck, and shoe.

_____

Write a sentence about molasses. Use exactly 8 words.

_____

© Evan-Moor Corp. • EMC 3394 • Critical and Creative Thinking Activities   137

Page 138

Sticky Stuff

Name _____

Which is better, glue in a bottle or glue in a stick?

Why? _____

Is it better to take off a bandage quickly or slowly?

Why? _____

In September, Penelope ate a peanut butter sandwich every Monday, Wednesday, and Friday. September started on a Wednesday. How many peanut butter sandwiches did she eat altogether?

13 peanut butter sandwiches

In September, Penelope's brother Henry ate a honey sandwich every 4th day. How many sandwiches did he eat altogether?

7 honey sandwiches

Emma keeps bees and sells the honey. She sells a jar of honey for $4.75. Yesterday, she sold twice as much honey as she did today. She made $133 dollars yesterday. How many jars of honey did Emma sell yesterday?

28 jars of honey

How many jars did Emma sell today?

14 jars of honey

How much money did Emma make today?

$ **66.50**

The answer is **try using some tape**. What is the question?

_____

The answer is **melted chocolate**. What is the question?

_____

138   Critical and Creative Thinking Activities • EMC 3394 • © Evan-Moor Corp.

Page 139

Sticky Stuff

Name _____

Sandy is the owner of Sandy's Candy, where she sells only yummy, sticky, sweet things. Use the price chart to answer the questions about what some of her customers bought.

Sandy's Candy

Caramel Corn	Small ...$2.50
	Large ...$3.75
Cotton Candy	...............$3.50
Marshmallow Squares	...........$2.25
Caramel Apple	...............$2.75
Saltwater Taffy	...... 12 pieces/$1.00

• Mrs. Garland has 26 students in her fourth-grade class. She bought 156 pieces of saltwater taffy to share with her students.

How much money did she spend? $ **13.00**

How many pieces of taffy will each student get? **6**

• Lewis bought 3 things. He spent $10.00 What did Lewis buy?

2 large caramel corn and 1 small caramel corn

• Janie also bought 3 things. She spent $8.25. What did Janie buy? **cotton candy, small caramel corn, and marshmallow squares**

• Coach Donovan bought a small bag of caramel corn for each of the 14 players on his soccer team. How much money did the coach spend? $ **35.00**

• You have $9.00. What will you buy at Sandy's Candy?

_____

How much money did you spend? $ _____

How much change will you get back? $ _____

© Evan-Moor Corp. • EMC 3394 • Critical and Creative Thinking Activities   139

Page 140

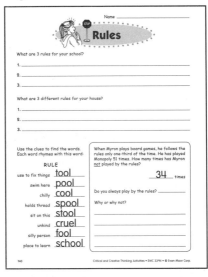

Rules

Name _____

What are 3 rules for your school?

1. _____
2. _____
3. _____

What are 3 different rules for your house?

1. _____
2. _____
3. _____

Use the clues to find the words. Each word rhymes with this word:

RULE

use to fix things	**tool**
swim here	**pool**
chilly	**cool**
holds thread	**spool**
sit on this	**stool**
unkind	**cruel**
silly person	**fool**
place to learn	**school**

When Myron plays board games, he follows the rules only one-third of the time. He has played Monopoly 51 times. How many times has Myron not played by the rules?

34 times

Do you always play by the rules?

Why or why not? _____

140   Critical and Creative Thinking Activities • EMC 3394 • © Evan-Moor Corp.

Page 141

Rules

Name _____

If you could make 3 rules that everyone on Earth would have to follow, what would they be?

1. _____
2. _____
3. _____

Use the clues to find things that have rules.

red and black squares	c**heckers**
place with books	**library**
place you swim	p**ool**
plan for eating	d**iet**
summer activity place	c**amp**
on TV	G**ame** **show**
word competition	**spelling** B**ee**

At Stephen's house, there is a rule that he can watch only 7 hours of TV a week. Last week, he watched 3 half-hour sitcoms, 1 movie that was two hours long, a football game that lasted two and a half hours, and a half hour of cartoons. Did Stephen follow the rule?

yes

Do you think that kids should have TV limits?

_____

What does it mean to "bend the rules"?

to make exceptions to the rules/ to not quite follow the rules

What is an example of someone bending the rules?

_____

Do you ever bend the rules? _____

© Evan-Moor Corp. • EMC 3394 • Critical and Creative Thinking Activities   141

Page 142

Rules

Name _____

Think about the rules for tic-tac-toe. How can you change the rules to make the game more interesting? You can change anything about the game, even the way the grid looks.

Write your new rules.

_____
_____
_____

Draw your new game. If you changed the grid, be sure to draw it that way.

Try your new game with a friend, and then write what it was like.

_____

Do you like the original game of tic-tac-toe or your version better?

_____

Why? _____

What are 3 other games that might be better if you changed the rules?

1. _____
2. _____
3. _____

142   Critical and Creative Thinking Activities • EMC 3394 • © Evan-Moor Corp.

Critical and Creative Thinking Activities • EMC 3394 • © Evan-Moor Corp.

Evan-Moor's
Daily Plan & Daily Record Books

Two must-have teacher resources with three fun themes to choose from!

Better together

Daily Plan Books include:
- *39 weekly lesson-plan pages*
- *Seating charts*
- *A class roster*
- *Places to organize important classroom information ...and much more!*

Daily Record Books include:
- *Record of Standards Assessed*
- *Assignments and Tests Forms*
- *Attendance Records*
- *Communication Log*
- *Student Roster*

Daily Plan Books

Organize your entire school year—and with style! Original artwork brings a touch of fun to these spiral-bound planners. 96 pages.

Daily Plan Book: School Days
All Grades   EMC 5400-PRO

Daily Plan Book: Garden Days
All Grades   EMC 5401-PRO

Daily Plan Book: Animal Academy
All Grades   EMC 5402-PRO

Daily Record Books

Finally, all the forms you need to track and record student progress in one spot! 96 pages.

Daily Record Book: School Days
All Grades   EMC 5403-PRO

Daily Record Book: Garden Days
All Grades   EMC 5404-PRO

Daily Record Book: Animal Academy
All Grades   EMC 5405-PRO

School Days

Animal Academy

Garden Days

Must-have resources that make learning fun!

A Word a Day

Help your students develop the rich and diverse vocabulary they need for academic success!

Research shows that strong vocabulary and word knowledge is directly linked to academic accomplishment. Make sure your students develop the rich vocabulary that's essential to successful reading comprehension and academic achievement with *A Word a Day*. Each book in this newly revised series covers 144 words in 36 engaging weekly units. And with new features, such as an oral review and a written assessment for each week, it's easier than ever to help your students develop the vocabulary they need.

Grade 1	EMC 2791-PRO
Grade 2	EMC 2792-PRO
Grade 3	EMC 2793-PRO
Grade 4	EMC 2794-PRO
Grade 5	EMC 2795-PRO
Grade 6+	EMC 2796-PRO

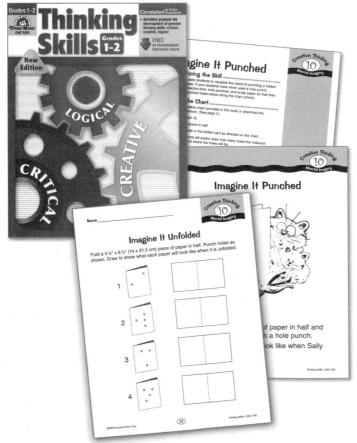

Thinking Skills

Help your students practice thinking skills with the creative and engaging activities in the *Thinking Skills* series. The 44 imaginative lessons in each book include downloadable interactive charts and reproducible practice pages to help your students think creatively, logically, and critically.

Grades 1–2	EMC 5301-PRO
Grades 3–4	EMC 5302-PRO
Grades 5–6	EMC 5303-PRO